Show Me the Way To Go Home

by

LARRY ROSE

ELDER BOOKS

Forest Knolls, California

Library of Congress Cataloging in Publication Data

Main Entry Under Title:
Show Me The Way To Go Home
Rose, Larry
1. Alzheimer's disease 2. Dementia 3. Health 4. Biography

LCCN 94-061038
ISBN 0-943873-08-8

Printed in the United States of America

Cover and Book Design: Bonnie Fisk-Hayden

Cover Photo Credit: The Image Bank

☾

I *dedicate this book to:*

My son Jeff and my daughter Rhonda;
Stella's daughter Stephene and her son, Jason;
and, of course, Stella. Without her memory, her tapes, notes
and especially her patience, I could not have written this book.

Also to my good friend Diana,
a fellow traveller through this labyrinth.

Table of Contents

"They that be whole need not a physician,

but they that are sick...

Go ye, and learn what that meaneth."

Matthew 9,
Verses 12-13

❨

INTRODUCTION

My father was an extraordinary man who led an ordinary life. In the early stages of his illness, my sister and I were ignorant about the disease. We did not want to know the truth. We sure didn't want anything like this to happen to him.

Let me tell you about the father I knew. He was an independent, witty, rugged individualist. There was nothing he couldn't do. He was the cleverest, funniest man I ever knew. When I was five, he would take me on jobs with him. Sometimes, they lasted for days. It seemed he knew everyone — I have seen total strangers stop him on the street and say, "Haven't I met you somewhere?" He always took the time to stop and talk to them.

He bought me a B-B gun one year, and he spent hours teaching me how to shoot it safely. He never advocated shooting at "those pesky sparrows." Instead, we always shot at paper targets. He taught me to read when I was three. One fish, two fish, red fish, blue fish — over and over and over. By the time I was 12, Dad had me flying airplanes. When I was 14, I skippered one of his tugboats during the summer.

Anything I thought I could do, he gave me the chance to do. "You can't learn any younger," he would say. No matter what happened, he would never hit the panic button. He was calm about everything.

Books were very important to him. It seemed he could never read enough. There must be over a thousand books in his cabin in the Ozarks. He has read every one of them. So have I.

He gave me a will to learn, and he made it fun. He always said, "If you like what you're doing, it's not work. I have never worked a day in my life."

Just two years ago, we rented a canoe and paddled down the Little Red River for 11 miles. We had to get out often and carry the canoe across the shallows. We would stop and sit on the bank of the river, talking like old pals. Dad laughed a lot, but always *with* you, never *at* you. It was a time I will always remember.

Now Dad is confused, frightened, and sometimes hostile and paranoid. He is, at times, completely dependent on aid from others. He has stopped reading, although I have seen him run his hands over the books on his shelves. He knows they are important, but sometimes he seems not to know why.

He has a hard time with language. At times, he can't form a sentence; his words are gibberish. Other times, you wouldn't know anything was wrong with him. He has courage, though. He pushes himself to the limit time after time.

Dad used to say, "Never indulge in worry or self-pity. It will tear down your personality and destroy your skills. The only thing that will make any situation work is the attitude you develop toward it." A true and valid maxim, I think.

My mother was killed in an auto accident in 1985. I don't think Dad ever really got over that loss. He talks about things they did together as if they happened yesterday. They were very close; we all were.

My dad is 58 years old, so young for Alzheimer's. To look at him, you would never know. He has an air about him that says, "I've got what it takes," without his saying a word. It radiates from him in letters ten feet tall. Like Will Rogers, he never met a person he didn't like... unless they gave him a reason.

Life growing up with him around was a kick. He worked at least 100 hours a week, every week, for as long as I can remember, yet he still had time for us kids. He helped with homework, Boy Scouts, baseball — everything. Looking back, I don't know how he did it. I still have a thirst for knowledge. I can thank both him and my mother for that; they made learning fun. Dad always said that a mind is like a tank with a slow leak; you must keep filling it up.

I'm grateful beyond words that he is my father, but I am frightened now at what is to come. I lost my mother when she was only 43, and now I'm losing my dad; but I feel lucky to have known him at all. Damn this disease! ☾

Jeff Rose

☾

Chapter 1

THIMK

An Unlikely Path Through the Perplexity of Alzheimer's

It was one of those days when everything was too perfect for anything unusual to happen. It was a day when you felt glad to be alive; one of those days when everything is right with the world, and nothing is wrong. I had no way of knowing that, before this day was over, a chain of events would be set into motion that would change "life as I knew it" — forever.

I was on my way to my mountain cabin in the Ozarks, near Clinton, Arkansas. It's a beautiful place, where one can get away from the rat race and the freeway mob. I try to spend as much time there as I can.

I had spent most of my life working in the service industry for what is commonly called the "Oil Patch." I was a special projects engineer for a small electric wire line company in Lafayette, Louisiana. A few years ago, I left the company and tried to unwind a little from the 12- to 15-hour days necessary to make it in the industry. When I wasn't spending my time at the cabin, I undertook consulting jobs, lobbying in Baton Rouge for some large, independent oil companies here in Louisiana, just to keep busy.

When I got to Alexandria, I stopped at a fast-food restaurant for a quick cup of coffee. I must have driven for about an hour when I realized that nothing looked familiar. I had taken this road for several years, and I knew it like the back of my hand.

When I finally got my bearings, I was near Shreveport, more than 100 miles out of my way. It must have taken two hours to drive that far. What had happened? What had I been thinking about during that time? The last thing I remembered for sure was stopping for coffee in Alexandria.

I made the necessary adjustments in my route to get me to Little Rock, where I would have to get off Highway 167 and take I-40 west to Conway. I knew then exactly where I was and where I was going.

As I drove on to Little Rock, I kept telling myself, "Larry, you must concentrate, try harder. What is wrong with you? Did you stop at all of the stop lights? Were you speeding?" I just did not know; I couldn't remember.

I was doing great now though, and as I drove, I carefully watched my speed and the traffic. It was such a nice day, and I was happy to be going for a respite to the cabin. It was then that I saw the sign "West Memphis, Arkansas." I must have taken another wrong turn in Little Rock. I should have arrived at the cabin by now. It was time for me to call my dear friend and long-time companion, Stella Guidry. I always called her when I reached the cabin, to let her know I had made it safely. It would take me another four hours to get to the cabin, and she would be worried sick by then.

I stopped at a pay phone and called Stella.

"So, you made it all right?" she asked.

"Well, no," I said. "I'm in Memphis."

"What in hell are you doing in Memphis?" she exclaimed, shocked. "I thought you were going straight to the cabin."

Not wanting to tell her what a stupid thing I had done, I said, "I decided to go see Graceland, since I was so close. I've always admired Elvis, you know."

We talked a little longer. She seemed satisfied that I was doing exactly what I had intended. I checked into a motel, ate a bite, and then went to bed, exhausted, afraid, and wondering what in the world was happening to me. Where there had been fear, now there was a cold, frightening emptiness.

I awoke refreshed early the next morning and drove on to the cabin without further incident. Over the next few days, I relaxed, watched TV, threw rocks at squirrels and tried to establish myself, in my own mind, as a "mild eccentric." I remember thinking while walking through the woods, "This must be where God lives," it was so beautiful.

I had bought a frozen pizza at the store when I arrived, so I decided, late one morning, to bake it. It was almost lunch time, anyway. I preheated the oven according to the directions on the box, placed the pizza inside, and checked the time. It was supposed to bake for 10 to 13 minutes and, as I waited, I looked out the window and noticed that the grass in the meadow was getting tall. Forgetting the pizza, I went out, started up the Ford tractor and began bush-hogging the two- or three-acre meadow in front of the cabin. I didn't think of the pizza again. Soon, I saw smoke coming from the cabin windows.

"My God," I thought, "the house is on fire."

I stopped the tractor and ran to the house to see if I should call the fire department. As I ran into the house, I realized that it was only the pizza burning. I never knew they could smoke so much.

It didn't take long to clean up the mess, air out the house and eat a cold hot dog. I vowed never to tell Stella about this incident. She would surely think that I was losing it. "I must concentrate harder on what I'm doing," I told myself. For the first time in my life, doubt stirred somewhere deep inside. It was unsettling and unnerving, and for a time, I felt the uncertainty of a person experiencing a hurricane or a tornado for the first time; the terrifying sensation that comes on realizing that what should be firm and solid is no longer so, and cannot be relied upon. I returned home to Louisiana a few days later. ₡

☾

Chapter 2

THE DIAGNOSIS

During the next few months, Stella kept urging me to talk to my doctor and long-time friend, Dr. Jim Trahan, about my memory loss, as there were more and more incidents indicating something was wrong. I kept putting it off, thinking that whatever this was, I would soon get over it.

Finally, Stella became insistent that I see the doctor. She was working in her office one morning and asked me to make her a cup of instant coffee. I went into the kitchen and looked around for a few minutes. Then I went back to her office and asked, "What is instant coffee?" She finally quit laughing when she saw that I was serious. It was then that she came unglued like a two-dollar umbrella.

"I'm going to make an appointment with Dr. Trahan right now. Something is terribly wrong with you, and I have had all of this absent-mindedness I can take."

"*You* have had all *you* can take? You should be looking at it through *my* eyes," I thought to myself. I knew I was in trouble, too, and I had no idea why.

The tests were scheduled for the middle of the next week. The MRI was the first on the list; then came the stress EKG; ultra sound on the carotids; a complete blood workup and then some X-rays. We got a call from Dr. Trahan a few days later, stating that all of the tests looked normal, but there were a few more tests he wanted to do, and he would schedule them later.

I was elated by the news from Dr. Trahan. I just *knew* that whatever was wrong was not serious; that it would soon pass. Maybe I just needed a few vitamins or a long vacation. "See, I told you, Stella. There's nothing wrong with me. My God, I'm only 53 years old."

A week later, I got my American Express bill and found that I had a $540 credit. Thinking American Express had screwed up, I showed it to Stella. She immediately called the bank and asked them to send my canceled checks early. Sure enough, I had written American Express a check for six-hundred dollars to pay a sixty-dollar bill.

The following month, Dr. Trahan called to tell Stella that I should see a neurologist. I had written him a check for six-hundred, seventy dollars to pay a balance of six dollars and seventy cents that the insurance had not paid. He said, "Not only is the check for the wrong amount and the date is wrong, but it looks like it was written by a ten-year-old. At this rate, Larry will be in a nursing home in less than two years!"

Stella made an appointment with the neurologist for a week later. I could hardly wait to see him. I just *knew* that it was nothing serious, and that he would prescribe a pill or something, and I would be all right in a few days.

The examination went well, or so I thought. He checked my reflexes, my vision, and my hearing. He had me read from a *Readers Digest* and then tell him the gist of the story. I thought I had done well, but I lost the thread of the story several times, and could only get back on track by prompting.

He then scheduled me for an EEG, and prescribed a mood elevator, saying, "The symptoms mimic chronic depression. If that's the case, the prescription should make a real difference to the memory loss." The EEG showed normal brain waves. Nothing wrong there, although I could not count backwards from 20. "Let's give the mood elevator a little time, and see how you are in a month," he said. Meanwhile, I want you to see a psychiatrist friend of mine. You'll like him."

We made an appointment with Dr. Ted Friedberg. After a short interview, he conducted a few tests that were confusing, to say the least. One, in particular, was a connect-the-dots puzzle not unlike the ones we did as kids. After two or three dots, I became confused. In exasperation, I took my pencil, broke it in two, threw it in the trash basket and said, "I'm through with *that.*"

Although my reaction must have seemed juvenile to Dr. Friedberg, he continued with a verbal test. "Where is White Sands?"

"New Mexico."

"Where is Brazil?"

"South America."

"What is the highest lake, in elevation, in the world?"

"Lake Titicaca."

"And what was the capitol of the Incan Empire?"

"Cuzco."

"Who was one of the presidents during the Civil War?"

"There was only one, if you are talking about the United States. I think Jefferson Davis was the President of the Confederate States. I can't remember who the President of the United States was — it just slipped my mind— but he was the one that got shot."

"But what was his name?"

"I don't know right now, but he gave a great speech at Gettysburg. You know, 'Four score and seven years ago...' I don't know why he didn't just say '87 years ago...' "

He smiled. "But, what was his name?"

"Uh... uh... uh... Lincoln."

"Right. Now, tell me, who were the last six presidents?"

"Let's see... before Bush, there was that actor; the peanut rancher; Johnson, and the one that got shot."

"Do you remember Nixon?"

"Oh, yes. I forgot about him."

"What do you remember most about him? Do you remember anything at all that made him famous?"

"Uh... uh... he chopped down a cherry tree?"

He tried hard not to laugh, but I could tell he was almost choking. When I'm under pressure to do well, it becomes harder for me to think. I had to smile too, though, when I realized what I had just said.

He continued. "Have you ever heard of the 'Four Horsemen of the Apocalypse'?"

"Yes."

"Tell me about them."

"Well, there was the White Horse, the Black Horse, the Red Horse and the Pale Horse." I went on to tell him the rest of the story.
"All right now... what did you have for breakfast this morning?" I couldn't remember, but I felt I needed to say something, anything. "Uh... chicken and dumplings, I believe."

He quickly excused himself and left the office. When he returned, he said, "I've spoken with the neurologist again, and he thinks it would be a good idea to do another test, called a 'Spectra Scan.' I've set it up for next Friday." He had me perform a few more tests. I was becoming tired and confused. I finally finished all the tests, knowing I had failed badly.

The doctor talked briefly to Stella in the lobby while I went to the bathroom. Stella said that he told her I knew all about the "Four Horsemen of the Apocalypse," but could not remember what I had for breakfast.

We drove home in silence. It was starting to dawn on me that I might be in serious trouble. The word "Alzheimer's" had not been mentioned at this point, but I knew a little about it from what I had seen on TV. Could this be my problem? No, I thought; only old people have Alzheimer's. I'm only 52. Or is it 53? Let's see, I was born in 1937, and this is uh... uh... what year is this? I turned to Stella. "What year is this?"

"It's 1992, Larry. Why?"

"Well, let's see... if this is '92 and I was born in '37, how old does that make me?" I was trying to subtract, but it just wasn't working. "You are 54, Larry. On your birthday, you will be 55."

"How long is it until my birthday?" I had no idea what month it was.

Slowly and painfully, I was becoming aware of the darkness in my mind. I realized that my mental abilities were fading and that I must work to overcome my fear of this loss. Everything that is important to me in life is slowly slipping away. Friends' faces, places and names are becoming harder and harder to remember. I am preoccupied with time and can never remember what time it is.

I try to face reality. Will I soon forget who I am? Is there a reason for all of this? Why am I living, if there is no purpose to life at all? Will I soon be leading an empty existence? No, I can't be thinking that. A life is never wasted. Even in this helpless state, there has to be a reason. I know that even in the most hopeless situations, there is still a possibility for growth. I must never lose sight of that.

I had tears in my eyes for the first time in years. Stella touched my arm. "Everything will be okay, Larry. We'll go through this thing together." Touch is so very important. It has become an art to Stella — how to touch and guide me. Will there be a day when touch is the only thing left?

The next morning, I decided to go back to the cabin. Alone in that beautiful place, I can think more clearly. Stella had marked my route on the atlas, and I drove there without difficulty.

I was driving a Ford Ranger pickup truck, a fine little truck for driving around town, but on a long trip, it was very uncomfortable. I made a mental note to get rid of it when I returned home, and get a more comfortable car. I must be getting old, I thought.

During the two weeks I stayed at the cabin, I spent lots of time walking through the woods and mountains. There is a waterfall about 200 yards from the cabin; it is roughly 12 feet high, and falls into a pool about 20 feet wide. The water is much too cold for swimming, but just to sit there and think and listen to the water is deeply soothing. The peace I was able to find there is like the peace you find in a church. I could have stayed there forever.

Stella called to let me know that it was time to come home for my doctor's appointment. I drove home the next day without getting lost. As before, the little truck took its toll on my back and legs, and I could hardly walk when I got back. The next day, I sold my pickup to a friend who had been wanting to buy it for some time, and I bought a Cadillac. I figured the bigger, the better. It was a beautiful car, and very comfortable; it also had lots of gadgets, buttons, bells, and so on. I never did learn how to work most of those things.

When Stella found out about the Caddy, she went through the ceiling. "Larry Rose," she said. "you already have one Cadillac convertible that you haven't driven in a year. Why in the world would you want to buy another one?"

I had, indeed, forgotten about the convertible. "I just wanted the neighbors to think we were doing well." What else could I say? "What you *need* is a pickup, and not another *little* one. I really don't think you should be handling your own affairs anymore."

I spent a day or two thinking about what she said and, finally, I had to agree. I was making some big boo-boos with my money. I made an appointment with our lawyer, and had her draw up a durable power of attorney, giving Stella the power to handle my affairs. It was one worry off my mind.

After we signed and filed the power of attorney at the courthouse, Stella told me, "Anything you want, just point at it, and it's yours; but please, be reasonable."

Needless to say, I didn't keep the Caddy very long. I put a "For Sale" sign on it and parked it at a friend's repair shop. It sold in a few days.

I took Stella's advice and set out to buy myself a big pickup truck. I soon found just what I wanted, another Ford — an XLT Lariat King Cab, with almost all of the buttons and whistles that the Cadillac had. I went home and told Stella that I needed a check to pay for the pickup, thinking that she would give me an argument. To my surprise, she wrote the check, handed it to me and said, "I think you made a great deal, Larry. It's just what you need. I don't know why you didn't get that truck in the first place."

I was a happy camper now, with my new truck, and with Stella handling my finances. She had all of my bills set up on the bank draft system, so we didn't have to worry about being late with anything. Now all I had to worry about was getting lost.

The good days were not to last long, however. Stella had asked me to buy her some thin copper wire for a stained-glass project she was working on. Boy, did *that* request stick in my mind. I bought a roll of copper wire every time I went to town. I must have had ten rolls of wire on her workbench when she finally realized what I was doing. Although she told me she had enough wire to last her awhile, that didn't stop me. I still bought a roll every time I thought about it. She finally took all the extra rolls back to the hardware store and got my money back. Then she told the salespeople not to sell me any more copper wire. After that, when I'd try to purchase copper wire, they'd convince me that I didn't need any more.

Meanwhile, some psychology students and professors at Louisiana State University had heard about my condition and wanted to give me some mental status tests. They were writing a paper for a medical journal and needed my help. They offered to come to the psychiatrist's office to give me the tests.

The tests lasted two days. I know I did well on some of the tasks they set me; but other things, a five-year-old could have done better. To form a simple design out of colored blocks was impossible, and to do some of the drawings was like trying to make a circle on an Etch-A-Sketch blindfolded. There were many other tests—including a math test which required me to count backwards by sevens. But the absolute pariah was connect-the-dots. I stared at it for a long time, but I just couldn't figure it out. I knew my five-year-old grandson could do it, and I could not.

I was glad when the tests were over. I was a nervous wreck, but I still didn't know what was wrong with me. The word "Alzheimer's" was never mentioned, although, down deep, I knew they were ruling out everything else.

The next few days were unbearably difficult. I couldn't get the tests out of my mind; I knew I had failed badly. Maybe I could take them again; if I were more rested, I could do better.

Finally, my last appointment with Dr. Friedberg came around. Although Stella and I went in together, he talked more to Stella than to me. There was talk of the frontal lobe, this lobe and that lobe. I had no idea what they were talking about. The word "frontal lobe" reminded me of a quotation that I'd heard a long time ago. *I'd rather have a bottle in front of me than a frontal lobotomy.* I smiled when I thought of that!

I had drifted off into Never-Never-Land, when Stella put her hand on my shoulder. "Larry, the Doctor is talking to you." I hadn't heard what he said. So, I asked him, "Is all of my brain rotten, or is some of it still good?"

"Much of your brain is still very good and working well," he said. "Will this memory loss last forever, or will it come back?"

"I'm afraid you must live with it," he said, very seriously. "You won't be able to work anymore. How are you fixed financially?"

"Well, I'm comfortable." I said. "I have enough money to last me the rest of my life, unless, of course, I want to buy something." He turned to Stella. "I would suggest you look into Social Security Disability."

"I've already contacted them," Stella said.

"Good. If there are any problems, tell them to call me."

As Stella drove us home, I looked at the papers that the doctor had given her. My eyes wandered to the bottom of the last page. "Dementia of the Alzheimer's type," it read.

There must be some mistake, I thought. This can't be. I am much too young. I don't even *know* anyone who has Alzheimer's. Isn't this terminal? This can't be. It can't. Why not something else? Something I understand? Something treatable?

I turned to Stella. "Do you think this is what I have?"

"I don't know, Larry. I don't know very much about this. But try not to worry. We'll find out what to do... how to treat it — what to eat, what vitamins you need. I'll get right to work on it. If there *is* a way out, we'll find it. Don't worry."

Right. *Don't worry.* That's like telling a convict on his way to the gas chamber to have a nice day. My world was crumbling around me. I had no place to stand. I had finally reached my limit. I was going crazy. Mad as a Hatter. I was there already. ☾

☾

Chapter 3

CONFUSION SETS IN

The weeks passed slowly. I had started carrying a notepad to remind me of important things. I read through it ten times a day and, so far, my notes showed I hadn't done anything stupid.

I found a paper in my pocket one day that read, "Don't forget to give Dr. Trahan back the key to his store." What in hell was I doing with a key to his store? Moreover, where *was* the key? "Maybe," I said to myself, "I just won't mention it, and he won't ask." So far, it's worked.

I am starting to have trouble finding the right words in conversation. Just today, I asked Stella. "Where is that sack of mushrooms?"

"What sack of mushrooms, Larry? We don't have any mushrooms, and anyway, I don't buy them in a sack."

"Sure we do, Stel. I saw them last night, the little, white, fluffy things in the sack."

"Oh, you mean *marshmallows*. They're up in the corner cabinet."

Poor Stella. She really has to stay on her toes when talking to me. Luckily, she is very adroit under pressing conditions. She has

learned quickly how to figure out what I mean when I ask something like, "Where is my brown thing (my comb)?" or, "Where is
the green stuff (mouthwash)?" Stella always knows.

One night, Stella asked me to sit down. "We need to talk." I hated
it when she said that, because it usually meant that I was in trouble. "What do you want for Christmas?" she asked.

"A tombstone," I answered promptly.

"What? What in the world are you talking about? You're not
going to be needing one of those for a long time."

"Yes I am. There is only one way to beat this thing in my head,
and that is to die. I'm not going to lie in a nursing home with my
mouth hanging open, like some Alzheimer's patients I've seen on
TV. I just need to find a cool way to check out, like skateboarding
down the side of the First National Bank building."

"With your luck, you would probably make the turn at the side-
walk and go down Jefferson Street at 200 miles an hour," she said,
with a laugh. "No, Larry. I buried my husband because of a drunk
driver. You lost your wife the same way. You know the pain. I
couldn't stand to do it again."

"Oh, no, Stella. This is different. I've had over 50 years of living.
Life has really been something, and I've loved every minute of it.
You and I have been through the jungles; we've seen monkeys
swing through the trees; we've climbed the pyramids and done a
hundred things that most people have never dreamed of. We once
saw an eagle fly. Remember?"

"Yes, I remember. "But I will grieve for you," she said, with a
sigh.

"Well, don't. When a person grieves for a friend, they are really grieving for themselves. I understand. *I* will be the one on the ship, sailing off to... God only knows what wonders; and you will be left standing on the shore, alone. I understand all of that Stella, but if you feel grief for anyone, feel it for the teenagers who died in that crazy war in Vietnam, or the young kids who have lost it to drugs, or the homeless in the cities. I'm sure you have heard the old saying, 'I was sad because I had no shoes until I met a man who had no feet.' If I die tonight, I won't be cheated out of much, Stella. I have done it all in my time, and life, so far, has been great. I have taught my little boy to bait a hook, and I had a little girl climb up in my lap and say, 'Daddy, I love you.' Who could ask more out of life?"

"I will still miss you, Larry. I love you!"

"I know, Babe. I love you, too. I'm sorry if I didn't realize that you are hurting over this thing, too. I'm afraid I was only thinking of myself. At least, I've had a *chance* in life. There are those who never had."

We held each other for a long time. I wished there was some way I could spare her the pain. "Will you promise me one thing, Stella?"

"Sure, Larry. What?"

"Will you have written on that tombstone, 'I would rather be here than in Houma, Louisiana!' "

"I think you mean it," she said, laughing.

The next morning, I went to Wal-Mart to pick up something or other... I forget what. I know it wasn't copper wire! I had taken Stella's Lincoln, because it was parked in front of my pickup. After 15 or 20 minutes, I came out of the store, but I couldn't find my pickup. I must have looked for over an hour, and walked past the

Lincoln ten times. I was beside myself, and dreaded calling Stella to tell her that someone had stolen my pickup. I was walking back to the store to see if I could find a phone, when an old friend and coffee-drinking buddy walked up to me.

"Hi, Larry. How you doing? I see Stella let you drive her car today."

I looked at the keys in my hand. They had Lincoln written all over them. "Oh, yes, I better head for the gas station. She only lets me drive it when it's out of gas." I was thinking fast. I was *thinking*. I was also very relieved. Now I wouldn't have to tell Stella anything. ❰

Chapter 4

TRUE FRIENDS

Knowledge, or the quest for it, has never been an insurmountable objective for me. Anything I ever wanted to know was easily obtained, either by asking an expert or by going to the library and researching the subject.

This strange disease that the doctors said I had was, indeed, unfamiliar to me. What I wanted desperately to know was, how long did I have to live? More to the point, how long did I have to live with some sense of what was going on around me? How long would it be before I became a vegetable? I had to find out, while there was still time.

I figured that the best place to go for answers was to the doctors. But I never got a straight answer from any of them. "How long have I got, Doc?"

"No one knows," was the usual answer. "Generally, the earlier the onset, the sooner you die."

"And where do you get that information?" I asked. "Statistics," they'd tell me, and then change the subject.

"Other than that, Larry, how do you like early retirement?"

Under my breath, I'd say to myself, *Other than that Mrs. Lincoln, how did you like the play?*

Not wishing to have what little intelligence I have left insulted further, I went to the local library. I soon found whatever books have been written about Alzheimer's, and I have read them all several times.

The 36-hour Day was about the best one I read. There was a lot of good information there, but it was mostly for caregivers. I could not see where any of it applied to me. I am just not like most of the Alzheimer's patients I read about. I can still think, talk, walk, write and do almost anything I want. Sure, there are times when I can't find a word I need; and yesterday, I stumbled. Stella tells me that I seem to be looking for something all the time. When she asks what I'm looking for, I answer, "Oh, nothing." She knows I'm not telling the truth; the fact is, I don't know.

Another good book was *The Diminished Mind*. It was written about a New England school teacher who was diagnosed with Alzheimer's in his early forties. I was moved to tears several times while reading it. I felt so sorry for him and, especially, for his wife, his caregiver. Again, I just couldn't see myself in him. He lived 15 or 16 years from the onset. Would I, as well? I don't want to, if my life hereafter is not quality life.

I spent several weeks at the library. When I had read everything I could get my hands on, I was still not satisfied. I wanted to learn more.

My father once commented that when I wanted to know anything, I would go after it 500 percent. When I finished my research,

I would know the subject inside-out, forwards and backwards, the benefits and the pitfalls. I suppose he was right. I was never satisfied until I knew all I could. I feel the same about Alzheimer's; knowledge about it is sketchy, and with knowledge about anything, there is less fear.

I decided to take Stella's advice and try anything that might help to delay the ultimate end— vitamins, diet, anything! I even thought of going to New Orleans and finding a Voodoo woman to make me a mojo to wear around my neck. I was desperate to try anything that might help.

I had not told anyone of my problems, except my sisters, Elsie and Lois, who still lived in Kansas, near where we were born. My brother, Cecil, who suffered a stroke several years ago, was not easy to talk to on the phone. I left it up to my sisters to keep him informed. My son and daughter had known from the beginning, but they took the attitude that if they just ignored it and didn't talk about it, it would go away, like the flu.

Afraid of how they would react, I tried to keep my illness from my coffee-drinking buddies. Dr. Trahan, of course, knew, but you couldn't get him to say anything about one of his patients if you held a gun on him. I don't know how my cafe friends finally found out, but I suppose it's like the old saying, "Three people can keep a secret if two of them are dead."

One morning, I joined all of them at our special table in the corner of the cafe. It was always the same bunch— Tyrone, Jim, Harvey, Bill, Danny, Curtis and Aaron. Dr. Trahan usually came only on the weekends. With his busy schedule, he just didn't have the time to stop for coffee very often. I had just sat down and said hello to everyone when I finally noticed that Jim was talking to me. "Larry, Larry, LARRY!!! Where are you, Man? We have been talking to you for five minutes. Your eyes look like glass, and you were just staring into space. Are you in Never-Never Land? Are you okay?" Finally, someone said, "It's this Alzheimer's thing, isn't it?"

"I suppose so," I said, wondering how they found out. "I would prefer to call it *The Enchanted Kingdom.*" But I wasn't fooling anyone — they all knew I was going through hell.

Their acceptance was surprising. They were all calm and cool. "Try not to worry, Larry. If you ever need help with anything, just let one of us know."

Later, Danny, a retired state police officer, told me that his dad, the former District Attorney, had recently died from Alzheimer's. He had helped his mother take care of him during his last years. He knew the symptoms, and he said he could tell I was in the early stages. "I don't know why you would want to hide something like this; you are still the same old Larry. Try to never forget that we're here to help you if you ever need it. Anything at all, just let one of us know."

I had tears in my eyes again. I was driven to tears more often lately. Was I becoming a softy? I had always heard, "Big boys don't cry." I wondered why people said that.

We all had one friend you could call special — Al Martin. One could not say enough about Al. I never met anyone who didn't like him. I had often wished that I could be like him. Al was fighting lung cancer; he'd contracted it about two years ago. He didn't come to the cafe much anymore, as he was spending more time in the hospital.

Every time I saw Al, he appeared to be thrilled, like we were old war buddies, meeting again after 20 years. He was not putting on airs; he was genuinely glad to see me. Al was a person you could talk to about anything, and for as long as you could talk. He took the time to listen. I guess that's what made him so special.

We would talk for hours about our respective illnesses, and about our ultimate end. He was a person who had never smoked and had always tried to eat the right things, but he still ended up with lung cancer. Al didn't understand it, and neither did I. He had recently lost Mary, his wife of 40 years. They had raised three adopted children, who were all grown up and married now, with kids of their own.

One day, after everyone at our table had gone, Al told me that he was quitting chemotherapy. He thought it was making him more sick than it was helping. He was living on pain pills, and I could tell that he was hurting.

"I feel like putting my Cadillac in the garage, shutting the garage door, rolling down the window, putting a nice tape in the player, and just going to sleep," he said.

"Al, I know how you feel. Believe me, I know. I've thought along those lines myself. I always thought the best way might be to take a cruise to Spain or France and go over the fantail of the ship in the middle of the ocean. But Al, please don't do it now, at least not until you talk to me first," I said, knowing that Al wasn't joking.

"When your time *does* come, Al, will you do me a favor?"
"Surely," Al said, with a smile. "What?"

"When you get to where you're going, and after you've said hello to Mary, would you look up Nancy (my late wife), and tell her that

I love her and miss her?" "She knows that already." Al said, smiling.

"Just in case. I never got a chance to tell her on the day she died." "I'll do it," Al said.

That was the last time I saw my old friend Al. He died about a month later, at home with all his children present. If it had to happen, I was glad it happened that way. I'm sure that Al has already done what I asked of him, and that makes me feel better.

What a much better world this would be if everyone had a friend like Al. I hope my memory never gets so bad that I will forget him. Memories of Al and the times we had together will always be a big part of my life. He was one of the special ones. God bless him.

I went to the cafe early one morning, shortly after it opened. When the waitress brought my coffee, she looked at me and asked, "Larry, are you okay?" "Sure." I said. "I just need my coffee to wake up."

When the first three or four people you meet ask you the same question, you begin to wonder. *Do I look or act differently?* I have trouble walking from time to time, and entering the cafe, I hold onto chairs or to counter stools until I get to the booth where we meet. I'm always relieved when I reach the booth so I can sit down. I guess it doesn't take a rocket scientist to figure out that I'm not walking too well.

As the news of my illness spread through our community, well-meaning friends would ask, "What are your symptoms?" I would try to explain. "Sometimes I can't remember the names of people or places. I can't find words that I want in conversation, and I'm always losing my keys or forgetting where I parked my pickup. I don't know which way to turn when leaving the parking lot. I can't make change anymore. I have to trust the cashiers to take the right amount of money and not shaft me. Things like that."

"Oh, don't worry about that," they say. "That happens to me all the time."

Sure it does.

I once made up the most incredible story, just to see what an acquaintance would say. "Last week, I was headed to the mall, and I got on the wrong road and drove for four days and nights, and ended up in Hartford, Connecticut." Somehow, I knew what the response would be. "That very same thing happened to me the other day. It's just a little memory loss. I wouldn't worry about it."

I will never know if these people are listening, or if they just want to make me feel that everyone does crazy things sometimes.

If that is all Alzheimer's is— a little memory loss, I would be a happy camper. The fact is that Alzheimer's affects the brain, and the brain controls not only memory, but reasoning, walking, sight and swallowing, as well as many other abilities.

One fellow in my neighborhood asked if anything I had been exposed to in the past might be responsible for my dementia. "I heard that Alzheimer's patients sometimes have a buildup of aluminum in the brain. Have you been cooking with aluminum pots?" "I read that aluminum buildup in the brain is a result, rather than the cause," I said, with authority.

"You mean that the brain might attract aluminum like a magnet?"

"Like a magnet? No. I would say more like mercury collects gold."

I could tell by the look on his face that I had lost him. He had no idea what I was talking about. I can't make myself understood anymore.

People need to be better educated about Alzheimer's. Most people really want to know; there are just no teachers. If only there was a way to tell them, without being arrogant, "Don't patronize me; I am not an idiot, although I now do some stupid things." I once had an I.Q. of 146. I know a high I.Q. doesn't mean anything now — I'm not sure it ever did. It doesn't make my coffee taste any better, and it doesn't make it any easier to cope with this disease.

I am becoming more and more withdrawn. It is so much easier to stay in the safety of my home, where Stella treats me with love and respect, than to expose myself to people who don't understand, people who raise their eyebrows when I have trouble making the right change at the cash register, or when I'm unable to think of the right words when asked a question. Maybe it would be easier for them if I didn't look so healthy. «

ℂ
Chapter 5

THE SLIPPERY SLOPE

I can feel myself sliding down that slippery slope. I have a sadness and an anxiety that I have never experienced before. It feels like I am the only person in the world with this disease. Although it has been over a year since I was diagnosed with Alzheimer's Disease, I have never met anyone else who had it. Could all this be a mistake? Could I have something else? Something treatable?

From time to time, I hear of an Alzheimer's patient; someone will tell me that Mr. Jones or Mrs. Smith has Alzheimer's. When I ask, "How old are they?" I always get roughly the same answer.

"Oh, Mr. Jones is 84," or, "Mrs. Smith died last year. She was 78."

I feel the need to talk to someone, anyone. But who? The unaffected experts are no help. Everything is either black or white to them. I cannot explain to them how I feel; the words are not there. Stella says that I am becoming more abstruse every day.

I feel that I am walking a precipice alone. No one understands the frustration in my thoughts. I must keep pushing myself to use the abilities I have left, pushing right to the end. How much further do I have to go? How long will it be before I reach that vast canyon of nothingness?

If I could only talk to my old friend, Al. He always seemed to know what to do or say. I can remember something he told me not long ago. He said, "Larry, you can sit in a rocking chair for the rest of your life, and just rock away, or you can stay busy. We're the lucky ones, Larry. We have a challenge every morning when we get up. We must never give up." Al did give up, though. He must have gotten tired of fighting.

The world is a little brighter, a little better because Al once lived. I miss him. I hope someone can say the same thing about me after I'm gone.

The letter from Social Security came today. I was afraid to open it; Stella looked at it first. I had been approved for the maximum benefits. It was the saddest day of my life. I am sure most people would have been thrilled, and maybe I was too, in a way, but it also meant that this thing in my head is real. Social Security doesn't just give disability benefits for the asking. They really do an investigation; they have good doctors at their disposal, who check every tiny symptom before making their decision. The whole process took just over 90 days. (I must add that I was treated with kindness and respect from everyone at the Social Security offices.)

My feelings could best be termed "bittersweet" about the news that I had just received. I didn't go outside for days. It was cold and cloudy. The sun wasn't shining. There were no stars in the sky at night. It was a dreary world. ⊄

☾

Chapter 6

LIMBO

My thoughts were on returning to the mountain cabin — I had a longing to get up there. But I din't trust myself to go there alone anymore, and Stella was busy right then with her accounting business. I thought my friend Aaron Dodge, a local electrical contractor, might be able to take a few days off and go with me. He and his kids love the place as much as I do.

He wired the place for me when I built it. I remember that weekend well. I told him that I only wanted two plug-ins in the whole house, one each for the refrigerator and the TV. He didn't listen to me, though. He and I ran a quarter-mile of wire — alarm systems, video cameras, switches and lights, plug-ins, stereo speakers and even spare circuits that I will never use. All of this in a cabin of 1200 square feet, including the loft.

Stella and I, Aaron and his whole family were there that weekend. We worked hard, but had a wonderful time. Since then, they spend about as much time at the cabin as I do. Aaron recently bought the ten acres across the "Holler," as the locals call it, and is planning to build a cabin of his own soon.

His youngest son, Kevin, who is five years old, calls me "Mountain Man," and I call him "Hill Billy." The smile on his little face would melt anyone's heart.

Aaron will sometimes say to me in jest, "Larry, you load the rifles up, and I'll put them dogs in your pickup truck, and we'll go over to Stone County and shoot us an opossum. We'll have them women folks make us an opossum gumbo."

What a wonderful life. I wish I had longer to enjoy it. It looks like I am going to have to squeeze a lifetime of living into the next year or two.

I called Aaron to see if he could get away for a few days. He was just too busy. Maybe around the next holiday, when the kids were out of school.

The days passed, or was it months? I have no perception of time anymore. The only bright times were the early morning hours at the cafe with my "cronies," as Stella called them.

The rest of the days, I spent alone in the house. If Stella had to be out during the day, she would call two or three times to see if I was all right. I would try to read, but I could not hold onto the story line for very long. I would reread a page two or three times and still not know what I had just read.

It was the same with TV. Stel and I could be watching TV on any given night, and she might say, "Larry, we have already seen this show."

"Not me, I've never seen it before. You must have watched it alone after I went to bed, or when I was in Arkansas," I would answer.

The truth is, I probably had seen it. I could watch the same programs over every day and still enjoy them. Reruns don't bother me.

I was telling the guys at the cafe about what had happened. "There is no such thing as reruns at my house," I said, with a smile. They all cracked up laughing. Curtis Bertinot, who has the auto repair shop where I sold the Cadillac, said, "Why don't you just buy one good movie on tape and watch it every day? Larry, think of the money you would save. Look on the bright side." Everyone laughed again, including me. Hell, it sounded like sage advice. It's always good to laugh. ❨

❨

Chapter 7

A MEDICAL BREAKTHROUGH ?

They say it's always darkest just before the dawn. It must be true.
Things couldn't have been darker for me at this time, but they were
about to change.

Stella got a telephone call one morning from Ochsner, a world-
renowned hospital in New Orleans. They were starting a new drug
study program for Alzheimer's patients and had chosen me as a
prospective study patient. They wanted to set up an interview to
see if I met all the qualifications. Talk about thrilled! I could finally see light at the end of the tunnel.

As the time of the interview grew nearer, I became increasingly
apprehensive. Doubts stirred about this strange new drug that no
one had ever taken before. What if it does more harm than good?
No one has ever taken it before. What about side effects?

Stella put my fears to rest. "Why don't we just go and talk to
them, and see what it's all about?" she suggested. "You don't have
to participate in the program if you don't want to."

She easily talked me into going. Then, I began to worry about the mental status tests they would give me. "I'll do anything they ask, except connect the dots, Stel. *Please* tell them not to ask me to connect the dots. I can't do it. There's no use trying."

"They won't make you connect the dots, Larry."

"Okay, I'm ready then."

We drove to New Orleans the night before my appointment. I was to be there at 9:00 a.m., and New Orleans is about a two-hour drive from Lafayette. We did not want to have to drive there that early in the morning, and then spend all day taking tests. It was too much to do in one day.

So we found a hotel, settled into our room, and then found the lounge. Stella ordered a glass of wine for herself, and one of those new, non-alcoholic beers for me, as I had quit drinking years ago. The band started playing, and we danced to a few numbers. It was the first time we had danced in months.

We got up early the next morning, ate breakfast, and drove to the Ochsner Clinic. Everything went according to schedule. Cheryl Benoit, the coordinator for the drug study program, gave me all of the mental status tests. It only took about two hours. She also interviewed Stella, while I was taking the tests.

The tests were quite similar to those I had taken before. I hoped I had done well enough for them to say that there was nothing wrong with me; that I should just go home and get a job. That was not to be the case, however. Dr. Strub, who was in charge of the study talked to me for a few minutes, looked at the tests I had completed, and said, "All right, you're in."

He told us that he would need to see the results of my previous tests, including the MRI and the Spectra Scan, and that I might have to take further tests to meet the requirements of the pharmaceutical company doing the study.

Stella told him she would take care of getting the test results for him. She got busy on the telephone and had everything faxed to him almost immediately. They set up another date for me to have a new EEG, some more blood work and X-rays. "There is no real hurry," they said. "We don't have the drugs here yet."

We drove back home, and I felt happy for the first time in a year. At least we were *doing* something. The effect of just doing *something* was enough to boost my morale.

The next morning, I was still feeling good and wanted to do something constructive. I told Stella that I wanted to build something.

"Like what?"

"A house, maybe."

"Well, we don't need to build a house, but there is a closet in the back bedroom that's too small. You could tear it out and build a bigger one!"

"All right," I said, as I started gathering up the necessary tools. I worked all day tearing down the closet, taking care to remove all of the nails in the two-by-fours and dispose of the old sheet rock and other waste.

I was back at it the next morning, working with gusto. Stella asked if I wanted a cup of coffee. "Sure," I said. "I've been worried that I haven't been getting enough coffee in my diet lately."

When she brought the coffee, I was sitting on a little stool, trying to pry a two-by-four off the frame of the door. Whoever built this house didn't spare the nails. She handed me the cup of coffee. I took a sip and leaned back on the stool. I leaned too far, and fell over backwards onto a board with a nail — the only nail I had not pulled out before I laid down the board. There is no need to tell where I hit the nail. Hurt? It could not have hurt any worse if I had been hit with a baseball bat, not to mention the hot coffee all over me.

I took a shower and changed into some clean clothing. It still hurt badly. Stella said that I should call Dr. Trahan to see if I needed a tetanus shot. I called his office, and told them what I had done. His nurse told me to come right on down and get a tetanus shot.

When I arrived, I told the receptionist that I was the one with the nail in my ass. It must have been the funniest thing they had heard in months, they were laughing so hard.

Then the doctor came in, and he was laughing too. "Everyone here is a comedian," I said with a smile, "but I am the one with the nail in my ass."

"You don't say 'ass,' Larry. The correct term is *gluteus maximus*," he said, still laughing.

"Yes, right... my gluteus maximus."

He looked at the wound. "Nail wounds can be bad. I'll give you some antibiotics, Larry. Take them for five days."

"Will do," I said, as I was leaving. "And another thing, I don't want to be getting a bill for this. You folks have had at least fifty dollars worth of fun from this thing, at my expense. I think you may owe me."

"Get out of here," he said. "I'll see you at the cafe in the morning."

Stella was waiting for me when I got home.

"What did the doctor say, Larry?"

"He told me that any work requiring the use of my gluteus maximus, for the next few days, is pretty much out of the question."

"In other words, he said to stay off your ass for the next few days?" she said, jokingly.

Being a creature of habit, I went to the cafe early the next morning. I don't walk too well, and with the pain of the injury, I had trouble getting around. Just opening the door and getting inside was an ordeal. As I walked back to our booth, I stumbled a time or two. I kept myself from falling by holding onto the backs of the stools at the counter. As I passed one of the booths, I heard someone say, "There's that old drunk again. He's in here every morning about this time."

When I sat down in "our booth," my friend Tyrone asked, "What's wrong this morning, Larry? You look sad."

I told him what I heard as I was coming in.

"Who was it? I'll kick his Goddamned ass all the way to the street!" He was getting up.

"Please sit, Ty. It's okay. Ignorance and intolerance is the hobgoblin in his head. Who better to ridicule than someone who can't defend himself?" I said, sadly.

"By God, *I* can defend you," he said. "if you ever need me."

"Let it go, Ty. There are stupid people everywhere you go. I wouldn't want to trade places with them. I would rather have what I've got."

"Well, all right, but you're a bigger man than me."

"Taller, maybe," I smiled.

I limped back to my truck after our coffee session, still wondering why it is that some people feel the need to make a statement like I heard this morning, when they have no idea what they're talking about. Don't they realize that things are not always what they seem? I thought back to a poem I once heard:

Today, upon a bus, I saw
a lovely maid with golden hair.
I envied her — she seemed so gay.
I wished I were as fair.

When suddenly, she rose to leave,
I saw her hobble down the aisle.
She had one foot and used a crutch,
but when she passed, a smile.

Oh, God, forgive me when I whine.
I have two feet — the world is mine!

And then I stopped to buy some sweets.
The lad who sold them had such charm.
I talked with him — he said to me,
"It's nice to talk with folks like you.
You see," he said, "I'm blind."

Oh, God, forgive me when I whine,
I have two eyes — the world is mine!

While walking down the street, I saw
A child with eyes of blue.

He stood and watched the others play;
It seemed he knew not what to do.
I stopped a moment, and then I said,
"Why don't you join the others, dear?"
He looked ahead without a word,
and then I knew he could not hear.

Oh, God, forgive me when I whine,
I have two ears — the world is mine!

With feet to take me where I go,
with ears to hear what I would know,
with eyes to see the sunset's glow,
God forgive me when I whine,
I am blessed indeed! The world is mine!

Author Unknown

Somehow, this poem seemed to fit my feelings just then.

Later that morning, we got a call from Ochsner. They had finally received the medicine for the study program, and they offered to send it by Federal Express, with the instructions. Since I was one of the first ever to take this drug, they would also send a list of possible side effects. "Don't hesitate to call or come to the hospital if anything at all unusual happens," they said.

The pills came the next morning. I could hardly wait to get started. I took the first pill and waited for something to happen. An hour passed, then two. I just knew I would be on top of things any minute now. How long would it take for this stuff to work? I tried to count backwards from 20. I couldn't do it. What did I have for dinner last night? I couldn't remember. These damn pills don't work.

Stella said, "Give them time, Larry. Pills don't work instantly. It may take months to see any improvement."

"I can't wait months. By then, I'll be crazy, sure enough."

"Well, just settle down and take the medication like the doctors prescribed."

It was hard to stick with the directions— I was tempted to take more pills to speed up the process. I always went by the theory that if a little does a little good, then a lot should do a lot of good. I told Stella my theory.

She said, "Suppose a recipe calls for one teaspoon of baking powder for a batch of biscuits. If you were to put in a cupful, you would just have a big mess. If you think your brain is screwed up now, just imagine what it would be like if you overdosed on this new medicine that no one knows anything about."

"I'm sure you're right," I said. "I guess I was just expecting too much."

The days passed slowly. It was time for my next appointment at the Ochsner Clinic. Stella and I drove over the night before, like we had done for the previous appointment. We stayed at the hotel and went to the lounge and danced, as we had done during the previous visit.

The next morning, we drove the short distance to the hospital and went through the usual tests — blood pressure, heart rate, ECG, and so on. They even videotaped a one-hour interview with Stella, me and one of the doctors — for future reference, they said.

The coordinator then introduced me to a pretty young woman of

Spanish decent, who was to give me the mental status tests.

"Hola! Buenos dias, bonita senorita. Como esta usted?" (Good day, Miss, how are you?)

"Muy Bien, gracias. Y usted?" (Very well, thanks. And you?)

"Muy mal. Tengo un problema con la mente!" (Poorly. I have a problem with my mind.)

"You speak Spanish very well."

"Muy poco. Necesito practicar." (Very little. I need to practice.)

"Si. Come this way."

She led me to her office, where she set about arranging things for the tests. She was so bright and comical that, on a different occasion, I would have laughed at all of the life and humor that I sensed in her.

But not now. Now, in her office, she had a gravity that I knew was not her normal way. She was all business now, as it should be. She held up several objects, one at a time, and asked me what they were — a comb, a doll bed, a watch.

Then we came to the scissors. "What do you call these?"

I could not think of the word. I knew what they were; I just could not remember what they were called. "Things to cut with," I said.

"Yes, but what are they called?" she asked. Silence.

"Come on. Tell me what they are called."

"One of us is forgetting why I'm here," I said coldly. "Let's move on to something else."

When the words were out of my mouth, I wished that I had not been so abrupt. She took it all in her stride, though, and went on with the tests. She was very professional.

The rest of the procedure went by without incident. I hated taking those things, as they were a constant reminder of how little I can do. There was a time when I could add a column of ten six-digit numbers in my head in less than a minute. Now, even the most simple math was too much for me.

I feel an anger, a rage inside my head. It is a defused anger, not localized to any substrata — it cannot be narrowed down to any one thing. Mostly, the anger is with myself.

My thoughts are tangled, not in any order. This is hard to bear, since my memory has always been excellent. I can recall when I could read a page in a book, any book, then read it back, from memory, six months later, word for word. I have done it often.

I once told my boss that if he ever wanted me to remember any-thing, he should tell me that it's important, and tell it to me slow-ly, and I would remember it, word for word, for as long as I live. So far, I can still remember things that he told me ten years ago, but I can't remember what I did yesterday!

Will there be a day when I won't even know who I am? The things that make me Larry? Will it matter then? The anger goes as quickly as it comes.

I think anger can be justified, at times. It's normal to be angry with Alzheimer's. It's a thief, a murderer, a destroyer of minds. I try to channel my anger in practical ways. The best way for me to do this is to write down my thoughts. Stella's word processor must be jammed by now. I write down my thoughts and experiences almost every day. Some day, my kids, or their kids, might want to know. If the words that I write don't make any sense, I mow the grass. We have the best-groomed grass in the neighborhood. Between writing and mowing, I have neither the time nor the energy for anger.

I try hard not to think of my problems, or why this has happened to me. Carrying a load of resentment inside can only be destructive. ◖

Chapter 8
FLOYD

I had been thinking of getting a pet of some sort. Pets can be wonderful friends. They'll give you unconditional love, if you love them back a little. They don't seem to care if you need a shave or if your hair has not been combed.

I happened to mention to my buddies one morning that I was considering getting a pet. My friend Jim said, "What kind of pet do you want to get?"

"A dog, I believe."

"What kind?" he asked.

"I don't know. A big dog, I think."

"I have a great idea," Jim said, after some thought.

"What's that?"

"What you need is a pig. You have time to spend with it, and you wouldn't believe what a pet a pig can make."

"A pig?"

"Yes, I had a pig once, and I have never laughed so much at a pet in my life. They're very smart. They learn quickly, and are no trouble at all to take care of."

"I must talk to Stella about this," I answered. "Where would one get a pig like yours?"

"I know a fellow who has a mama pig. She just had nine babies, and they should be ready soon."

I talked to Stella about the pig when I got home.

"A pig?" she asked. "What kind of pig?"

"I think they call them 'potbelly' pigs."

"If you want, Larry, but a pig will take some getting used to."

With Jim's help, I soon had my pig. I named him Floyd. He was solid black and weighed about eight pounds when I brought him home.

Floyd was a joy. He was housebroken in two days. I found he would do anything for a jellybean. He would shake hands, roll over, and stand up on his back legs and beg for a jellybean like a dog. He would sit beside me on the couch and watch TV for hours.

Floyd became my constant companion. He went everywhere with me. He would ride in the passenger seat of my pickup and look out the window. Floyd almost caused accidents when passing drivers realized that there was a pig in the front seat of the pickup. They've often done double-takes.

Floyd often went with me to the cabin. When we'd stop for gas, a crowd would gather around to watch him do his tricks. A woman school teacher we met at a service station was so impressed with Floyd that she wanted me to show him to her second-grade class. I did, and the kids were thrilled. They fed him candy, bananas, and an assortment of food from their lunches. Floyd ate it all with gusto. They spoiled him, I think.

At the cabin, Floyd was like a kid, roaming everywhere. He especially liked to root around the base of an old elm tree beside the cabin that had not yet succumbed to blight. There must be something about the roots that taste good to him. He had the ground around the tree plowed up faster than I could have done with a rototiller. The ground looked like it was ready to plant a garden in when he got through.

Floyd didn't like the cold weather, though. When it got cold outside, he would bang on the door with his snout until I let him inside. Then he'd get under the castiron potbelly woodstove and sleep for hours. I sometimes worried that he might be getting too hot, but the heat didn't seem to bother him.

Life with Floyd is a joy. We roam through the woods like a couple of kids, stopping now and then when Floyd finds something good that he wants to root up and eat. When the weather is hot, he goes down to the creek and sits in the water to cool off. At home, he sits in his water bowl.

He loves to play, but I must watch him constantly. If I take my eyes off him for just a minute, he will run between my legs, get in front of me and spin around two or three times. I'm not as nimble on my feet as I once was, and he's knocked me down a few times; it's just the way he plays. He knows what "no" means, but he doesn't like it. When I tell him "no," he quits and walks away, squealing in protest.

I have learned to love Floyd. I wouldn't trade him for a dog or any other pet. ☾

❨

Chapter 9

STELLA

Regrettably, as I sink further into this progressive, degenerative disease, Stella must take the additional measures that are proving necessary. It seems easy for her to anticipate unpleasant eventualities and correct them before it's too late. However, she always handles exigencies with uncanny rectitude. I got lost twice last week while on my way to morning coffee; so Stella bought me an I. D. bracelet and a wallet card explaining my illness, in case I ever got into real trouble. We also had a telephone installed in my truck. She programmed it to automatically dial her, Aaron or Jim (all of whom offered to help, if the need ever arose), just by punching in one, two, or three, respectively; then "send." "Just as a precaution," she said.

It wasn't long before I had to use my cellular phone to call Stella. I was on my way home from a dentist appointment. The thing wouldn't work. The screen where the telephone numbers are displayed said "locked." I had never seen that before, and I must admit that I don't know much about cellular telephones. I thought I had ruined it, so I drove at once to the place where we bought it and went inside to explain the problem. The technician told me that the problem was not serious. "All you have to do is dial in the three-number unlock code, press "send" and it will unlock."

"Three-number code?" I asked.

"Yes, your three-number code."

"I don't know anything about a three-number code," I told him. "We never did put in a code."

"All right. What are the last three digits of your phone number?" he asked, in an unctuous and insouciant tone.

"Gee, I don't know."

"You don't know your phone number?" he asked, in disgust. "God, where do you people come from? The nuthouse must be full," he said, with obvious irritation.

Deliberate rudeness is something I detest, whether it is aimed at me or someone else, and deliberate rudeness is what I was getting. He pushed one of the buttons four or five times and said, "Here is your number." After unlocking it for me, he walked away, without a word.

I drove home, hurt, and wondering what I had done or said to deserve such treatment. Why does one feel the need to deride a fellow human being?

Stella sensed something was wrong and asked what had happened. When I told her what I had just gone through, she had fire coming from her eyes.

"Let it go, Stel. Everyone has burned toast for breakfast once in awhile. I just feel sorry for his wife. *I* will never have to see him again. *She* has to live with him 24 hours a day."

Later that day, we were watching TV. The store where we bought the phone was running an ad. "Look, Stel, what a needless waste of money, advertising on TV. They could still count on me as a customer, for only a smile and a few kind words."

I never kick. I never nag. I never criticize. I just don't go back. My life is too short to engage in a scrimmage for the sake of a couple of bucks.

I can't say enough about Stella. She is a true friend. With her, you can dare to be yourself. You can say what you think and express what you feel. She is shocked at nothing, offended by nothing, so long as it is genuinely me. She understands the contradictions in my nature that lead others to misjudge me. With her, I can breathe easy; she understands. Best of all, I can keep quiet with her; it doesn't matter. She loves me. I love her. She has a personal appeal and an easy affability to everyone who meets her. She has class!

Class is hard for me to explain. Kennedy had it. Nixon did not. I think class can best be described as someone who gets out of the shower to take a leak.

However, I *can* write my name in the snow. ◖

((

Chapter 10

LOST IN A MAZE

It was time for my next appointment for the drug study program at Ochsner's. This was to be a short one — just an interview with the coordinator and a visit to the lab to have some bloodwork done.

Early that morning, I told Stella that I wanted to go by myself, because it wouldn't be a lengthy visit, and I was feeling very good. She reluctantly agreed, as this was her busy time of the month with the accounting business. She reminded me that Harvey or Jim had volunteered to go with me any time.

However, I decided that I would try to go alone.

I made it to the city with no problems, until I left the parking lot and rode the elevator down to the lobby. When I stepped off the elevator, I might as well have stepped onto the moon. Nothing was familiar. The halls were all different.

None of the doors were in the same places. I walked through a door which I thought would take me to the elevators, and found myself outside. I really panicked then. I walked back inside and down one of the halls. There were bilingual "No Smoking" signs everywhere; the "No" was outlined in red, no doubt to give extra substance to the word. I knew that I had to go to the clinic on the sixth floor. I found the elevators but, somehow, they were different, and I couldn't figure out how to get to the sixth floor. I was still about a half-hour early. "Don't panic," I told myself. "Act normal." There was an information booth nearby, and I asked the attendant for directions. After studying my appointment card for a moment, she asked, "Are you an Alzheimer's patient, here for the study program?"

"Yes."

"Where is your caregiver?"

"I came alone," I answered proudly. "It might have been a mistake, though."

"Okay, just take one of those elevators, any one of them, and be sure to get off on the sixth floor, and take this card right to the desk." She pointed toward the elevators.

"Any one of them?" I asked, unsure.

"Yes, any of them."

I went into the lobby and waited for the elevators, still unsure of myself. I got into the next available elevator. The button for the sixth floor was already lit, so I didn't bother punching it. The car stopped on almost every floor, finally coming to the sixth. Someone in the elevator said, "This is the sixth floor," although I don't remember asking anyone. I got off, walked to the desk clerk and handed her my appointment card.

"Am I at the right place?" I asked.

"You sure are. I'll tell Cheryl that you're here."

Cheryl came out and got me right away. She asked how I had been and where Stella was. I told her that I had come alone, of the problems I had in getting here, and that everyone was so nice in helping me find her office.

As before, she checked my weight first thing. "About the same — 182 pounds," she said. "That's good."

We then walked down the hall to her office. She asked a few questions about any problems I had experienced during the past month. I answered as I remembered. Then she hooked me up to the blood pressure and heart-rate machine and punched in the necessary buttons. After checking my blood pressure, she was alarmed. "Your blood pressure and heart rate are up more than 30 points. I should ask Dr. Strub about this."

She came back in a few minutes and said, "Dr. Strub thinks the rise in pressure and heart rate are just because you had a hard time getting here this morning. He wants you to lay down on the examining table for 20 or 30 minutes; then we'll check your pressure again, and see if there might be a difference. You're alright here, you're safe. Just relax; try to sleep, if you can." She closed the door when she left the room.

I lay there relaxed. I could hear the ringing of distant telephones; the sound of people in the hall seemed to come from everywhere. I caught the smell of a disinfectant, although I couldn't quite place exactly what kind it was. I was tired and must have dozed off. This Alzheimer's is hard work.

I was startled when Cheryl came back into the room.

"Let's check that blood pressure now." She set about getting everything ready again and took the tests a second time. When the thing quit beeping, she smiled. "Back to normal, one-twenty over eighty. The pulse rate is sixty-two. That's better than most people your age. You'll be okay. Just relax, go down to the second floor, and get your bloodwork done. Here's a supply of pills for next month and your appointment card. Your next visit will be lengthy, by the way, so bring Stella with you." *A nice way of telling me not to come here alone anymore*, I thought to myself.

I got back home without further incident, talking to Stella from time to time on the cellular phone. About every 30 minutes, we would call each other. That way, I couldn't get too far off the beaten path.

That night, after dinner, I sat down rather hard on the couch. The couch slid backward a little, and one of the wooden legs broke off.

Stella said, "Larry, look what you've done. You broke the couch. You shouldn't sit down so hard."

"Well, it wasn't me, Stel. The leg just got caught on the avocado floor tile, and broke when it wouldn't slide."

"Terra cotta, Larry."

"Yeah, right... terry avocado."

"Well, you should be more careful when you sit down. Now we'll have to get it fixed."

"Look, Stel, I'm 50... uh...something... years old. I may not know how to sit on a couch, but I'm not going to take lessons. How about if I just buy a new couch? Unless you have a lot of ... uh ... sediment value attached to it."

"Sentimental value, Larry."

"Right... Sentimental."

We fixed the couch and did a good job. It's still hanging in there. ◖

☾

Chapter 11

FEAR & ANGER

I went to the cabin alone again. It seemed that the Arkansas winter was hanging in longer that year. The cabin is high on one of the Ozark Mountains, in a coppice of white and red oak trees. All of the trees were bare, with the exception of the pine and cedar that were scattered throughout the woods. I awoke early one morning and dressed with care, since it was cold. Was this a day to wear boots? There was no snow outside. I might just wear my Nikes.

I made a pot of coffee. I still had not made up my mind whether or not to wear boots. I got them out of the closet and wiped them down. Small decisions were becoming difficult to grapple with; big ones were impossible. I knew all of the signs; I could feel them coming on, but there was nothing I could do about them. I went to the kitchen to get another cup of coffee. It was all gone. Had I drunk the whole pot? I must have. I'm the only one here.

I'm going crazy, I thought. No, I'm not going crazy. I'm safe here. I'm in danger here. Should I wear my boots? Should I not? Back and forth went my thoughts. I would mislay my keys or my wallet, or lock myself out of the house. For some arcane reason, I would set my alarm before I went to bed, then forget to shut it off when I got up the next morning, thus setting off the warning buzzer when I walked into the kitchen. Once the buzzer is activated, I only have 20 seconds to punch in the numbers before it automatically calls the sheriff's department. I punched in the numbers like a madman. I finally got it shut off — just in time.

I finally decided to wear the boots and drive to town to buy supplies. It's 16 miles to Clinton. I found myself in Conway, 40 miles further down Highway 65. The people at the gas station here must love me. I tell myself, "Think, Larry, think. You can't let up, even for a moment." There is just no telling what crazy things I might do.

In the days that followed, I found myself in a complex and variable mood. I was not at peace, but was filled with determination to get a grip on this thing in my head. I turned on the TV, hoping that if I could get interested in a program, it might put my mind to rest, at least for awhile. The set was tuned to the local PBS station. *Bradshaw on Homecoming* was just starting. I had heard of Bradshaw. I knew him to be one of the all-time great counselors. I watched for over an hour, with great interest. He was holding a workshop for people who were trying to find and deal with the "inner child." Some of the people in his audience were sobbing; others were very angry, mostly with their parents. I thought back, like he suggested, to my childhood, and tried to find the "little Larry."

My mind raced back to when I was about four years old. I was wearing a cowboy suit that my mother had bought me through a catalog. I was a happy little camper, running through the barn, the corral, and even the chicken house, shooting all the bad guys with my new six-guns. Then there were Hop-A-Long, Gene and Roy, with whom I could ride the range while they were looking for outlaws. I always spotted the outlaws first. I hate to say it, but Hop-A-Long, Gene and Roy were slower on the draw than I was.

Letting my mind drift through my childhood, I could never find anything to be angry or sad about ... not as far as my parents were concerned. I guess I was one of the lucky ones. The only reason that I was ever angry with my folks was, through no fault of their own, they were old. It was my brother, who was 11 years older than me, who took me fishing and hunting. It was rare that my father ever did; he was always busy with farming, ranching and, later, politics.

All in all, I'm grateful to Bradshaw. I'm glad that, perchance, I turned on the TV that day. I had met a neat little kid, this "little Larry." I would like to hang out with him again, take him fishing, maybe even ride that range with him and catch those bad guys.

One evening, I got a telephone call from a friend who knew I was at my cabin. He was telling me what a tough day he'd had on his job; it had been a busy day and he had made several mistakes. "If *you* have Alzheimer's, *I* must have a *double* dose of it," he said.

I could feel myself entering a state of rage. "Do you forget simple words, or substitute inappropriate words, making your sentence incomprehensible? Do you cook a meal and not only forget you cooked it, but forget to eat it? Do you put your frying pan in the freezer, or your wallet in the sugar bowl, only to find them later and wonder what in the world is happening to you? Do you become lost on your own street or at the mall, not knowing where you are, or how to get back home? Do you forget how to dress, sometimes wearing three or four shirts? Do you mow your lawn three or four times a day? When you balance your checkbook, do you completely forget what the numbers are and what needs to be done with them? Do you become confused or fearful ten times a day, for no reason? And most of all, do you become irate when someone makes a dumb statement like you just made?"

"No."

"Then you don't have Alzheimer's," I said, and hung up. I was becoming hateful and execrable. It's not my nature, and I despise myself for it. but I can't understand why people make such statements. I must watch myself more closely. I don't have so many friends that I can afford to lose even one. Why couldn't I have said, "Yes, it looks like you had a bad day," and changed the subject? A year ago, a statement like that would not have bothered me.

I sat down in my overstuffed recliner. The silence was growing like a cancer. My thoughts were jumbled, and nothing was making any sense. *Maybe some music,* I thought. I put in a tape of Tchaikovsky's "Piano Concerto Number One" by Van Cliburn.

The music was interrupted by the telephone. I decided not to answer, to just let the machine take it, but my curious nature got the better of me. I ran to pick it up. "Hello," I said, thinking it might be the person who had just called.

"Hey, Dad ... glad I caught you in." It was my daughter, Rhonda. "Stella told me you were at the cabin."

"Well, hello, Baby Doll. What's new with you?" I asked.

"I just needed to ask your opinion on something."

"What's that, Darling?" I was happy again. At least she valued my opinion.

"I've been looking at new cars. I found a Chrysler convertible that I like. I just wanted to see what you thought about it."

"Well, as you know, I have had several Chryslers that we used for company cars in the past. I don't recall having any real problems with them. As far as I know, they make an excellent car," I said.

"I just wanted your opinion before buying it, since it costs a lot of money." She sounded worried.

"Look, Baby, you work hard. You need to enjoy life a little when you have time off. You *are* going to keep your pickup to pull your boat, aren't you?"

"Oh, yes! I don't think I'll ever sell the pickup. I love that truck. There are a lot of memories in it," she said.

"Do you have enough money to pay for it all, with the tax and license fees, too?"

"Sure."

"Don't run yourself short just to buy a car."

"We're in pretty good shape," she said. I could hear the pride in her voice.

"Then I would go ahead. Make the best deal you can. Argue a little. Cry if you have to. Then offer them less than they're asking. See what happens."

She laughed. "Okay, Dad. I'll do it. You take care. I love you. Bye."

It was getting late and there was nothing much on TV. I'm limited in the number of programs I can pick up out here in the woods.

I awoke early the next morning, made my usual pot of coffee, and sat down by the window facing the hollow. The sun was still behind the mountains to the east. Puffs of fog hung in the hollow like smoke on a battlefield. I had the feeling it was going to be a great day.

Movement in the hollow caught my eye. Four deer were making their way up the western slope of the hollow. I ran to the bedroom to get my camera. What a great picture they would make, if I used the telephoto lens. When I got back to the window, they were gone, like the puffs of fog in the hollow. Something must have startled them. Another time, perhaps.

Just last summer (or was it the summer before?), there had been a mother bear and two cubs hanging out in the hollow near the creek. There were a lot of wild berries down there, and I spent hours watching them eat and play. I didn't have my camera with me then. What a pity.

Later that same morning, I heard a noise that sounded familiar, but I couldn't quite place it. "I know I've heard that sound before," I thought to myself. I was becoming upset; I couldn't figure it out. About that time, the answering machine picked up the call, and I realized that the sound I couldn't identify was the telephone ringing. Such a simple thing to everyone else, but not to me... not on that day.

I ran to pick up the phone. It was my old friend, Ken Williams. He and his wife were passing through and thought they would stop to see how I was doing. They needed directions to get to the cabin. I pulled a hand-drawn map out of my wallet that I kept there "just in case," and read him the directions. I put on another pot of coffee for them, and waited.

It wasn't long before they pulled up in the driveway. When Ken came to the door, he gave me a big hug.

"This is from Stella. She told me before I left that if I ran across you, to give you a big hug."

"All right!" I said. "Please come in."

I led them through the house, showing them everything. We went upstairs through the loft and out to the cantilevered balcony that overlooks the hollow and creek below. I told them about the deer I had just seen and about the bear cubs last summer.

"This must be what heaven is like," Ken said. "I think so," I answered.

"This is just great, Larry. I didn't expect to see a place like this out in the mountains. Sunken bathtub, mirrors from floor to ceiling, and that rug in the loft is fabulous."

"Dr. Trahan gave me that rug. When he sold his big house and moved, he didn't have room for it anymore, so he gave it to me."

I poured their coffee and opened a sack of donuts. "How are you coping with your illness, Larry?" Ken asked, with concern.

"I'm doing okay. I can't do all of the things that I once could, but I get by. I've learned a lot of little tricks to cover up when I goof."

"Just asking, Larry. I don't want you to take this the wrong way, but... have you ever talked to God about this?"

"Sure. All the time. I have come to realize that, even though God created the universe and all of the things in it, there are certain things that even God can't do."

"Come on, Larry. Name me one thing that God can't do."

"Well, for one thing, He can't make pi come out even. He can't change the number of degrees inside a circle to be more or less than 360. It might be the same with this Alzheimer's thing. It might be that He couldn't change it even if He wanted to. He may have created Alzheimer's the same time He created those daffodils that are blooming outside right now. It might be part of the scheme of things, part of a much greater plan than we can ever know."

"I never heard it put that way before. I can't argue those points with you, Larry. You have such insight. I could never have put those thoughts into words," he said.

"Well, Ken, I have time to think now. Believe me, I think about dying a lot. There has to be a line drawn somewhere ... when it is time to go, when life is not quality. I would rather die six months too early than six months too late. I hope, when my time comes, that I can find someone like Dr. Jack Kevorkian. If I can't, I'll do it myself. The "do-good" groups and the government have to get over their love affair with terminally ill people. Unless they are in my shoes and those of millions of others like me, they have absolutely no idea what they are talking about. I want to live as much as the next man, Ken, but not lying in some nursing home, not knowing who the hell I am. I think Eddie Chiles said it best: 'I want the government to do three things and only three things — protect our shores, deliver the mail on time, and leave me the hell alone.' " Ken nodded.

"I don't think there is anyone on this earth who knows better when it is time to check out than the person who is dying. I sure don't want anyone in Washington, or some do-gooder in Utah or Alabama, or anywhere else, telling me that I *have* to live, any more than I should tell someone in California that she can't have an abortion. It just taxes the imagination. Sorry, Ken, I didn't mean to get on my soap box."

"It's okay, Larry. I couldn't agree with you more." We talked for a long time. They decided that they had to be going. I told them of a scenic route they should take. It was a dirt road, but there were cliffs two or three hundred feet high; "The Little Red River" runs through it. We said our goodbyes, and they drove away. The phone was ringing again. It was my son Jeff, although I didn't realize it right away. "Hey, Pa. This is Jeff."

"I have a son named Jeff, but he lives a long way from here."

"Dad, this *is* Jeff."

"I know, son, I was just joking," I lied. "I haven't seen you in such a long time."

"How are things with you? Are you still going to school?"

"Things are not so good. I got bucked off a horse while showing off, and broke my tailbone. I'm in Canada. I'm still in school, although we're on break right now. I've been 'running the roads,' looking around."

"Running the roads? Does that make you a 'roads' scholar?" I joked. "Hey, right. I'll tell my girlfriend that I'm a 'roads' scholar. She'll love it. I *did* tell you about my new girlfriend, didn't I?"

"No. What happened to the little German girl that you were hanging out with for the last few years?"

"As the song goes, 'She's about as gone as a girl can get.' I think they wrote that song for me."

"When will you be finished with school, Jeff?"

"I'll finish next year in either London or Paris."

"That will be great, Jeff. You must have more degrees than a show dog."

"Well, with that and a dollar, you can buy a cup of coffee."

"I thought you were going to become a professional student. You've even outdone your sister. She just graduated last year; I think she was 28."

"Yes, I have her by four years."

"It takes more than education to make it in this world, son. I heard a story one time. The man who told it to me swore it was true. Want to hear it?"

"Sure."

"In England, during the War, there was a man who lived in London. He worked at a church; he cleaned up, kept things organized, and rang the bell on Sunday. His only problem was that he couldn't read or write. After the War, the church elders decided that they were going to upgrade their staff and that they couldn't have someone in their employ who was illiterate. They gave him six months to learn to read and write. Try as he might, he just couldn't make it. They fired him, and he went home and told his wife.

'What are we going to do?' she asked.

'Well, I've always wanted to open a tobacco store. We have a little money saved up. I would like to give it a try.'

He opened his tobacco store and did very well. Within ten years, he had a dozen stores throughout England, and had amassed over a million pounds. While at the bank one day, his banker told him that he wasn't getting all of the benefits of having a large sum of money. He should have it working for him in stocks and investments.

To make a long story short, it finally came out that the man could not read or write. 'I don't believe it,' said the banker. 'Man, do you realize where you would be today, if only you could read and write?' 'Oh, I know exactly where I would be,' said the man. 'I would be ringing the bell over at the church.'

"So, Jeff, I think you can see what I mean. It takes more than education. A lot more. Like Howard Hughes — he didn't worry about losing a million dollars on a venture. If he lost that million, there was another million out there somewhere. A lot of people start out saying, 'I can't,' and it ends right there. Attitude, enthusiasm, risk and, of course, education — they all play a part."

"You don't need to worry about me, Dad. *Can't* was never in my vocabulary."

"I know, Son. I never worry about you. You can make it."

"Thanks, Pa, for the words of wisdom. I'd better hang up now or I won't be able to pay Ma Bell." I hung up the phone, then immediately called Stella to tell her about my day. I am not too nimble at making phone calls anymore, and I must have dialed at least three wrong numbers before I finally reached Stella. On one wrong number, I got someone in Tampa, Florida. He was a nice fellow, and we talked for about an hour before I hung up. "Don't you think it's about time for you to come home?" Stella asked. "I can't right now. They're predicting a foot of snow tonight. I don't want to be out driving in that."

"I guess not," Stella said. "Do you have enough firewood and food?"

"Oh, sure. I have the heat pump that Aaron installed the last time he was up here. So I really don't need any wood, unless the electricity goes out, and I have enough food to last for a week or two."

"Well, stay as long as you want. Aren't you getting lonely?"

"No. I've had the telephone screwed into my ear all day. I might have to take out a bank loan to pay the bill. Then, of course, there are Tricksie and Bubbles ..."

"Tricksie and Bubbles?"

"The two new maids I hired."

"I'm coming up there this weekend, Larry, and that house better be clean," she said, laughing. "I love you, you nut."

"Ditto, Stel." We had a total of 16 inches of snow that week. I burned some serious wood. When the snow melted away in a few days, I was on my way back to Louisiana. ☾

Chapter 12

A WORLD-FAMOUS PIG

I had just gotten back from the cafe one morning, when Stella reproached me. "You are going to have to do something with that pig, Larry," she said, with some disgust.

"What's the matter, Stel?"

"Yesterday, he came home with a crowbar, and I don't know where he got it. We don't have a crowbar."

"I think you're right. Deena (our next-door neighbor) saw him walking down the street the other day, carrying a shovel in his mouth. I don't know where he picked that up, either."

"Well, it has got to stop, Larry. The neighbors have been tolerant of him so far, but if he keeps bringing their things home, they will get upset."

"He's not going to *hurt* the things, Stel. I think most of the neighbors like him. They always stop and talk to him when they're out jogging."

"I know what you're saying, Larry, but you can't have him roaming the neighborhood, picking up anything he likes. How would you feel if someone's dog ran off with your lawn mower?"

"Okay, I'll take care of it. I'll go down to the feed store and get a fence-charger and some wire. I'll fix up something to keep him in the backyard."

I spent the next few days wiring up the backyard with some thin steel wire on insulators, and plugged it into a small electric charger. It wasn't long before Floyd touched his nose to the wire. You could have heard him squealing for a block. He ran to the middle of the backyard and stood there for an hour, his tail sticking straight out and the hair on his back standing up like a mad dog's. He learned his lesson well. Thereafter, he wouldn't come within ten feet of the small wire. He also wouldn't have anything to do with me for two or three days. Somehow, he knew I was the one who did this to him. I finally got back on his good side with the jellybean treatment. He'll climb a *ladder* for a jellybean.

I really hate to hurt him. He has been such a companion. Stella says that if I go to the cabin without him, he just lays by the back door and cries until I get back.

Floyd is getting to be a world-famous pig. Just the other day, I had occasion to talk to a bank in Ohio about a Visa account. When we finished our business, the lady on the phone asked, "By the way, how is Floyd?" I didn't know what to say. I wish I had asked how she knew about Floyd, but I was so dumbfounded, I just said, "Floyd is well. I'll tell him that you asked about him." I hung up, still wondering how the knowledge of Floyd got all the way to Ohio.

It wasn't long before I got a card from a doctor in Oregon. He asked for a picture of Floyd standing up on his back legs, begging for a jellybean. Stella sent him one, along with a letter asking how he knew about Floyd. So far, we've received no answer. ☾

☾

Chapter 13

LAUGHTER HEALS MANY ILLS

Some time ago, we received an information package from the Alzheimer's Association. In one pamphlet, there was information about a new program called "Safe Return," a nationwide, community-based safety net that helps identify, locate and return individuals who are memory-impaired. The program provides an identity bracelet or necklace; clothing labels and wallet cards to identify the individual; registration in a national database, and a 24-hour, toll-free 800 number to contact when an individual is lost or found.

Although I have a wallet card and an identity necklace, Stella thought it would be a good idea to register in the new program. They provided an application, which asked for a lot of information, including addresses and phone numbers of friends and family.

Stella was too busy to attend to the application just then, and it lay around for a few days without either of us looking at it further. One afternoon when I wasn't doing much, I decided to fill in as much as I could. I worked on it for about an hour, then put it aside.

A week or so later, I told Stella that maybe she should finish the application and send it off to the Association. She looked at what I had filled in. I have never heard her laugh so hard in all the years I have known her.

"Larry, what sex are you?"

"What a silly question, Stel," I answered.

"Where the application asks for 'Sex,' you put 'None,' " she said, still laughing.

"They want you to be truthful, don't they?"

"Yes, but you're going to give us a bad image by being *too* truthful!"

"You know, that reminds me of the employment applications I used to get. One lady who was applying for a secretary job wrote down under 'Sex,' 'Only one time, in Baton Rouge.' Another fellow wrote 'Yes' under the question 'Salary desired?' I hired him. He was the only employee I had who knew exactly what he wanted."

We laughed until I could hardly catch my breath.

"Well, I am going to change your answer to 'Male.' "

"Sure. I don't even remember that question," I said, truthfully. "You know, all this could be for nothing."

"Why do you say that?"

"I'm not sure I have Alzheimer's. It might be something else."

"Larry, at least ten neurologists, one psychiatrist, a medical doctor and the entire staff at LSU's psychiatric school say you do."

"Maybe they're all wrong. Maybe I got bit by a tsetse fly or something. I'm a Libra. Maybe my planets are just out of whack. It could be the creeping crud." If there are four million Alzheimer's patients in the United States, why have I never met one like me?"

"They're there, Larry. You just don't find them at the cafe."

"Why not? If *I* can go to the cafe, why can't *they*?"

"It's a big world, Larry. Not all of them live here."

"Just *one*, Stel. All I want to meet is *one*."

"You will ... someday."

"I'm just going to quit worrying about it. You'll see when I get well."

"Don't count on it too much, Larry. It may never happen."

"Oh, Brenda said she saw you at the library yesterday, and that she talked to you for awhile."

"Oh, yes! I remember," I lied. "A pretty girl looking for a book." I figured that would make sense, at the library.

"What were you doing at the library, anyway?" Stella asked.

"Library? Oh, I was looking for a book on how to cook an opossum. I have one in the oven right now. I've been watching *Yan Can Cook*, but to no avail. At what point do you put in the potatoes?"

She failed to see the humor. "I can never get a straight answer from you," she said.

I went out to feed Floyd. He was carrying a screwdriver in his mouth. I swear, I don't know where he gets all that stuff, but maybe I could train him a little. "Buick, Floyd... bring home a Buick." ❰

☾

Chapter 14

THE ILLEGAL SYSTEM

As much as we would like our friends to be honest, honorable and forthright, in reality, that is not always the case. Some remain true to their word, while others take advantage in every way.

My two kids and I have a rental property. I have had it rented since shortly after my wife died. In the first stages of dementia, I had completely forgotten to collect the rent for several months. When Stella started looking after my affairs, she asked me about the property. I told her that I thought I sold the place long ago. When she looked into things, she found that the renters had been depositing the rent checks into my bank account every month, right on time. This posed no real problem, except that my bank records were really messed up. That didn't bother me since I felt I was okay as long as I came within a few bucks of balancing my checkbook. A few dollars short one month, a few dollars over the next. No problem.

This house affair, and some other things, are some of the reasons

Stella sought medical help for me in the beginning. The point is, the renters could have taken advantage of me, and they didn't.

On the other side of the coin, I had loaned a friend and prominent businessman, with whom I'd worked for many years, some money. Twenty-thousand dollars, to be exact. His wife had sued him for divorce, and she had all his money tied up in court. He had a business to run and a payroll to make. Although I didn't ask for one, he made out a note, payable on demand, at eight percent interest. I told him that I trusted him, and that the note was not necessary, especially the interest. He insisted. He said he would pay me back as soon as he could get the courts to release his accounts.

I had known and worked with this man for years, and I knew him to be a successful and astute businessman. I knew his wife and children. I had lunch and dinner with all of them a hundred times or more. I would have trusted him with my life. I'm glad now that I trusted him with my money, instead.

When you try to merge two households, each of which has been established for 20 or more years, there is quite a bit of "stuff" — things that bring memories to mind when touched, held, or moved about. Inside each of us lies a memory bank of our lives; and these little things seem to trigger those memories, bringing out the best and, sometimes, the worst in each of us.

That particular day, Stella and I were sorting through and packing household effects to ready my house for the new tenants. Nancy's presence was everywhere. Stella began to get a new insight into this lady who had shared my life for 27 years, especially in the "little" things — things that meant nothing to anyone else but Nancy. Her initial N on a pin; a small, dainty handkerchief with her name embroidered on it; her first nursing patches from school; a wedding cake decoration with a man and woman; even a little dimestore pin with the words, "Greatest Nurse in the World" that one of the kids had bought for her when she graduated.

"This was a life," Stella thought aloud. "These things should go to Rhonda." They would not mean anything to anyone except a member of Nancy's family. She gently picked up these little items. "I'll put them away for a while, Larry. Later, when I have time, I'll create a collage of some sort."

"That would be great, Stel. Rhonda should have them. Things don't mean much to Jeff. He's not much of a person for 'things'."

Jeff is a different kind of person. He won't spend more than six or seven hundred dollars on a pickup truck. When it won't go anymore, he junks it and buys another six- or seven-hundred dollar truck, and goes on.

I asked him one time, "Jeff, why don't you get yourself a new truck?"

"I don't have to impress anyone."

"Right on," I said.

Jeff was born out of his time. About 200 years. He is more like Daniel Boone or Davey Crockett than anyone I know. Although he is well-educated (still in school at 32), he is more at home in the woods or the mountains of Colorado, or chasing wild horses in Wyoming, than in a crowd of people.

Meanwhile, I had boxed up quite a few things and had loaded both the car and the truck, and we were on our way to Stella's house. We stacked and stashed boxes, one by one, deciding what to keep here and what to take to the cabin. Stella grabbed one of the boxes and yelled to me, "God, Larry, what do you have in *this* box? I can't even lift it out of the car."

"That's old silver coins and gold...for a rainy day ahead."

"Yeah, right...just what we need...to get robbed! You need to get a safe deposit box for all of this stuff."

"No way. I don't trust banks with safe deposit boxes. I would rather put it where I can dig it up whenever I want it. Look, it would take a box as big as a washtub."

We proceeded to open the boxes of coins and began looking for a stronger box in which to place all of these items.

While we were transferring the coins, Stella discovered an envelope tucked away in the box. "What's all of this?" she asked me.

"Huh? I don't remember. Let's open it. I think it's the papers for the dog."

"Yes, Maggie's papers are here, but there is also a note, payable to you, Larry, for twenty thousand dollars, at eight percent interest. Has it been paid?"

"No."

"It's a demand note, Larry — payable on demand."

"Well, I have already demanded. He said he would pay me when he was damned good and ready. I guess he's just not damned good and ready."

"You may have to take legal action. This note will prescribe in a little while."

"Not really, Stel. See that six hundred-dollar payment? That extends the prescription for another five years."

"Okay, I'll put it aside and give it to our lawyer when we get settled in."

The following week, Stella made an appointment with Lisa, our lawyer, and we proceeded to try to collect this long-overdue note. I knew it would take awhile; twenty thousand dollars, however, is not something you just throw away.

Lisa sent the demand letter for the note, plus interest. It was something like twenty-nine thousand, less a six hundred-dollar payment.

The response was: "The demand is too vague and ambiguous to respond to. Does the payment apply to the interest or principle?"

Our answer: "State law requires that payments of this sort must be applied to the interest."

"We will stipulate that the payment must go to pay the interest, but my client didn't pay a payment at all," was their answer.

Stella went back through my bank records and found where a deposit was made into my account on the date that appeared in the payment section of the note. The bank made a copy of the check and deposit slip for her.

"That was a gift," was their answer.

"Let the court decide," I told the attorney.

They petitioned the court for a motion for "Judgment on Exception of Prescription," and a court date was set.

The day of the hearing, the judge called the attorneys into his chambers before the trial started. It seems that my adversaries had taken him to dinner a day or two before. He offered to excuse himself from the case. We thought it was just one of those things people do from time to time and that the judge could still listen to the evidence and render a fair verdict. So we told him that we thought the dinner thing would pose no problem, to go ahead with the hearing.

I testified first. It didn't take long for the defense to jump onto the Alzheimer's thing. "Isn't it true, Mr. Rose, that you have been diagnosed with Alzheimer's?"

"Yes."

"Isn't is also true that you sometimes can't remember things, and that you get lost going from your home to the cafe?"

"Yes."

"Isn't it also true that you didn't remember your street address in the deposition?"

"Yes."

"Isn't it also true that my client paid the note in full, and that you just don't remember?"

"No. If something is emotional, I can remember."

And so it went. When the defendant went on the stand, he was magnificent. It was obvious that he had been on the stand before. He had the answers down pat. Yes, he had paid me about six months after I loaned him the money. He paid me in cash. Yes, I gave him a receipt, but he threw it away (this is a businessman who handles millions of dollars a year). The six hundred-dollar check paid to Larry Rose? That was a gift, because Larry's such a nice fellow.

I never thought for one minute that the judge would buy it. When it was over and the judgment was read into the record, I couldn't believe it.

The judgment was as follows: "When, after hearing the evidence and argument of counsel, the Court, being of the opinion that the law and evidence are in favor of the Defendant and against the Plaintiff, for the reasons orally assigned and, accordingly, the exception of prescription filed by Defendant is sustained.

"It is, therefore, ordered, adjudged, and decreed that Plaintiff's suit against the defendant, in the above-captioned matter, be, and the same is, hereby, dismissed, with prejudice, at the Plaintiff's cost."

When we left the courtroom, Lisa said to me, "I'm sorry, Larry. I can't believe the judge ruled that way."

"It's okay, Lisa. You did your best. That's all I could ask of anyone."

"But, Larry, *twenty-nine thousand dollars!*"

"It's not going to make me, and it's not going to break me. What about an appeal?"

"That judge was just voted the best in the state. They won't even look at an appeal."

"Well, let's just go home and cry, then."

On the way home, Stella said to me, "I can't believe it, Larry. All of the evidence was on your side. They had nothing."

"It's a matter of politics, Stel. I told the truth; my adversaries took the judge to dinner. See how it works? Truth and lies get clouded over all the martinis. Don't worry about it. There is a higher court that takes care of things like this. God will be looking into this thing. Someone once said, 'You have done me an injustice, but I am not going to sue you; the courts move too slowly. I am going to *ruin* you.' "

"Remember what God said, Larry... 'Vengeance is mine.' "

"Yes. Let's put it to rest. When he dies, the money will be put to good use — his kids can use it to hire mourners and pallbearers."

"Just don't ever mention his name again."

"It'll be hard. He was once my friend. But I am more upset over our justice system — we don't have a 'justice system' — it's a 'legal system.' No, let me change that; it's an '*ill*egal system.' I can't get this dinner thing out of my mind. Maybe I should have kissed the son-of-a-bitch."

"Do you have trouble with the words 'what, when and where,' Larry?"

"Yes. Those are hard words for me to get straight in my head. If you ask me, 'When did you get back from the cafe?' I might say, 'On Johnston Street.' "

"I thought so. That might be why the judge ruled against you. You were sometimes hard to understand."

"Maybe there should be a court just for Alzheimer's patients. My advice for persons afflicted with any memory impairment would be to stay out of the courts. If you can't talk, you can't win. You know, I always believed that the police were our friends, that they would help us if we ever needed help. Now, we have all seen a video on TV of a group of cops beating the hell out of a man in California. Then they say that what we saw is not what we saw. The FBI and the ATF declared war on a group of citizens in Waco, because they thought differently than most of us. Frankly, I would rather be protected from the FBI than from a bunch of preachers. There once was a time when you could trust the system to do the right thing, but not any more."

"I don't think you will ever get over this court case, will you?"

"No! There's an old saying, 'Feed a starving dog, and it will never bite you.' Apparently, there is a *big* difference between a man and a dog."

"I heard that one of the court clerks asked the judge how he could have made such a decision, and the judge answered that 'Larry wasn't emphatic enough,' " Stella said, after some thought.

"Hell, I don't even know what that means."

"Emphatic?...Assertive, expressive, insistent."

"So what you are saying is that when he said that he had paid me in cash and that I had just forgotten, I should have stood up and yelled, 'Liar, liar, pants on fire,' and I would have gotten my money?"

"No, No, No, Larry," she said, laughing. "Just not so many, 'uh...uh's."

"I can't help it, Stel. Sometimes the words won't come. I'll keep that in mind, though, the next time I loan someone twenty thousand dollars, and they don't pay me back." ❰

☾

Chapter 15

DIANA

Now and then, if you're lucky, you meet a person who changes your life. You can know people your whole life and never be friends. You can know someone for five minutes and be friends for life — such was the case when I met Diana McGowin. I first saw her on a TV show called *Prime Time Live*. I watched with great interest, and I told Stella, "This is the first time I have ever seen someone with Alzheimer's who is just like me. We are exactly the same age, and were the same age at onset. We can still walk, talk and, with a few exceptions, function in society. I have just *got* to meet her."

The next day, I called Information in the city where she lived. To my surprise, the operator gave me a number right away. *The number is probably for some other Diana McGowin*, I thought, but I dialed it, anyway. The worst that can happen is that she won't want to talk to me, or that I have a wrong number.

She answered.

"You don't know me," I said. "Are you the lady with Alzheimer's?"

"Yes, I am," she said.

"Well, my name is Larry Rose. I am the same age as you, and I also have Alzheimer's disease."

"Well, I am glad to meet you, Larry. We are traveling the same road together."

We talked for two hours about everything under the sun, "from soup to nuts," as the old phrase goes. We went over, in great detail, our lives — from when and where we were born, through our being diagnosed with Alzheimer's, and on to the difficulty of coping with this disease. It was almost like we were twins, separated at birth.

She talked to Stella for a few minutes before we finally hung up.

In a few days, I received a letter from Diana. She said how great it was hearing from me — that most of her phone calls were from people who had just been diagnosed with the disease and were depressed. Diana told me I had turned the tables on her and that she had a smile on her face for days after our conversation.

We still keep in touch, and we exchange letters, phone calls and videotapes. I sent her a video of Stella, and of Floyd standing on his back legs, begging for a jellybean. In turn, she sent me a videotape of her house and the surrounding area, including the jetties she loves so well. Whenever I'm feeling down, all I have to do is put her videotape in the player and, within minutes, I'm laughing like a fool.

During one of our conversations, she asked me if I had fulfilled all of my goals in life. "I never had any goals, Diana. I only had dreams."

"Only dreams? I don't understand."

"One can change dreams, Diana, but one can never change a goal. For example, I always had a dream that one day I would go to Peru and roam through the rainforest — jungle, really; rainforest is just a nice name for a jungle — and search for Incan ruins. I had that dream until I got there and took a look at that jungle. I awoke from that dream in two minutes. No one in their right mind would venture out into that place. Now, if I had been an archaeologist with a goal of getting the job done, I couldn't have given up. I would have had to go on. My whole life has been dreams, Diana, one after another. When you get to the point where you have more regrets in life than dreams, you're finished."

Diana encouraged me to write, and to keep pressing myself to the limit. Through her, I have met at least ten others like us — people with early-onset Alzheimer's, from age 42 to their late 50s. I haven't met them in person yet, but we correspond regularly. I don't feel alone anymore, and the emptiness in the pit of my stomach is gone, thanks to Diana. I know that I have made a friend that I will have as long as I live. ❰

☾
Chapter 16
Big Sleep

It was one of those mornings when everyone was in a good mood. I was a little late getting to the cafe, and Dr. Trahan was already there with the rest of the group.

"You're late, Larry. Try to make it on time from now on," said the doctor, jokingly.

"I never get to the cafe before I wake up, Doc. I know it may sound silly, but it's just a little rule I have."

"I haven't seen you in a long time, Larry. How are you?" he asked.

"You know how, when you lean back in a chair and you almost fall over backward, but you catch yourself at the last second, and you don't fall? Do you know that feeling?"

"Yes."

"I feel that way all the time."

"Man, you're in bad shape. I think they have surgery for that sort of thing. I'll ask around. And how is your sex life?"

"I'm holding my own," I said. Everyone cracked up.

"Whatever it is that Stella is feeding you, tell her to keep it up," someone quipped.

I don't think I ever laughed so much in my life. Living was good that day. Nat Schmulowitz, a lawyer/writer/historian, put it best when he said that humor can be more interesting than straight stories, and it can tell more about a person. "A vain man, a bigoted man, or an angry man cannot laugh at himself, or be laughed at. But the man who can laugh at himself, or be laughed at, has taken another step toward the perfect sanity that brings peace on earth and good will toward men."

This is a true and valid maxim, with one exception: an attempt at humor that misses *really* misses.

When I got back home, Stella told me that she was going to Hawaii for a few days for a workshop, and asked me if I wanted to come along.

"No. I think I might go down to Belize for awhile and jog over to Teotihuacan while I'm there. I've never been there, and I want to see those old ruins before I die, and while I still have a little bit of sense."

"You can't go down there alone, Larry, to another country. You might get lost."

"I'm not completely helpless, Stel. What if I *do* get lost? No one stays lost forever. I have friends in Belmopan, if I need help."

"I would rather you didn't go until I get back. Please wait, and I will go with you."

"Okay. I'll just mosey up to Kansas, and see my brother and sisters while you're gone."

"That sounds better. At least I can call you now and then, to make sure you're all right."

"Done deal."

"We need to do a lot of things around here before we go, Larry. You'll need to find someone to take care of Floyd."

"I can take him with me."

"Okay. We need to pick all of those grapes and do something with them soon."

"Can't do that."

"Why not?"

"Floyd ate 'em."

"Damn it, Larry. *All of them?*"

"Yep. Green ones, too."

"Even the ones way up on top?"

"Yes."

"How could he have gotten the ones on top?"

"Hey, you know Floyd. He can climb Italian marble, if he wants up there bad enough."

"Damn that pig!"

"Don't be mad at him, Stel. He likes grapes."

"So do *I*, damn it!"

"But *he* can't run down to the store and buy them like *you* can."

"I wouldn't bet on it. Aside from that, we still have a lot of things to do before we go."

"Right. What if I die before you get back? Should you tell someone to just put me on ice for awhile?"

"Get off that dying kick, Larry. All I hear from you is, 'When I die, when I die...' "

"What should I say? 'Demise'?"

"Eternal rest, maybe."

"How about, 'bought the farm,' or 'down for the count'?"

"Good. What's wrong with, 'pushing up daisies'?"

"Happy Hunting Grounds."

"Big Sleep."

"Debt of nature."

"The Great Adventure."

"I cashed in my chips."

"Quietus. Bit the dust."

We both laughed like we were nuts. "No matter what you call it, Stel, the ultimate end is six feet down, toes pointed up." ☾

☾

Chapter 17

THE COMFORT OF FRIENDS

Days rolled by like a slow train. I took Stella to the airport and drove on to the cabin. I decided to rest there for a few days, and then drive on to Kansas, where my brother and sisters live. We bought a program for the computer called "AUTOMAP," which is really a boon to Alzheimer's patients like me.

You just enter your present location and your destination into the computer, and it prints out a detailed map and a log. It tells you the roads to take, where to turn, what direction to take and, of course, the mileage. It even notes the time it should take from city to city, if you can still make sense of a clock.

Early one morning, after talking to my sister, and armed with my AUTOMAP, I left the security of my cabin and started driving to western Kansas. I thought that if I got tired or confused, I would just stop at a motel and rest for a bit. That had always worked for me in the past. It's not like I'm on a schedule.

It was late in the afternoon when I reached the panhandle of Oklahoma. God's waning interest in the countryside had become more and more apparent as I traveled further.

I didn't remember everything being so brown — no grass or trees, just brown prairie. I once lived here. It seemed so long ago, yet some memories of my childhood flashed through my mind like they had happened yesterday — hunting coyotes and jack rabbits with my brother; the pet skunk we had out at the farm (Old Doc Pierce had de-scented him for us. He'd charged something like two dollars).

I suppose I was happy here. I couldn't be now. Everything is so barren. You can look further here, and see less, than anywhere I have ever been.

I missed my sister's street and ended up on McCall Street. Thinking that was the proper street, I drove up and down three or four times. The houses didn't look familiar, and I moved over a block, to Maxwell Street. I found the house right away. They met me in the driveway. It's a good thing they did; I couldn't walk. I had been in the truck so long that I was stiff and sore all over. Sy, my brother-in-law, helped me inside. I had forgotten to bring my cane.

"You came to visit at just the right time, Larry. The high school alumni is having a banquet and dance next Saturday. Can you go?" my sister asked.

"Yes. Great. It would be good to see some of my old friends," I answered.

We talked for a long time, taking a break to eat and watch a video I had brought of Floyd. I bored everyone with stories and pictures of Floyd. I was moving around a little better by now, and it was getting late, so I decided to take a shower and go to bed.

I stepped into the shower. Something was not quite right. The shower didn't feel like it should, but I couldn't tell what was wrong. Oh, well; maybe it would come to me later. I found the soap and started to lather myself. How stupid. I had taken off my pants, but not my shirt and shorts. I took them off quickly and finished my bath. I wrung out the shirt and shorts, hung them up in the bathroom to dry, and hoped they would be dry by morning, so my sister would not know; and then I got into bed.

I got up early the next morning, dressed, and made a pot of coffee. Lois, my sister, came in, and we talked for awhile. Later, we went down to the cafe, where everyone in town gathers each morning for coffee. I guess every town has its cafe. The farmers were bitching about the weather, and the ranchers were bitching about beef prices. Some things never change!

Lois and I said our goodbyes to everyone and we went for a drive out into the countryside. We drove out to the old ranch where I was born. Nothing was left but a few trees and, of course, the Cimarron River that runs nearby. They say it is dry most of the time nowadays. The old Santa Fe Trail is still there; you can see it in a few places. It brings back old memories.

We drove on over to Liberal, to visit Nancy's grave. I don't mind going in the spring or summer, but I never go there in the wintertime. Everything looks so cold and desolate there then. I can't stand to think of her there, in that cold and lonely place.

Saturday finally came. We all went over to the school early in the afternoon. People were gathering in groups and talking. It had been so long since I had been there, I didn't know many people anymore.

I wandered outside to smoke my pipe and think. Suddenly, my old friend and classmate, Denny Quinby, drove up. God, it was good to see him. It startled me when I first saw him; he's the sheriff there now.

We talked over old times, and he brought me up-to-date on what was happening. We hopped in his car and drove down to the filling station for coffee. We sat at one of the two booths they had at the station.

"Where is Stella?" Denny asked.

"She's in Hawaii," I replied.

"You didn't go with her?"

"Oh, no, Dennis. It's just too far."

"I wish she would have asked me to go. She might need a body guard," he said, with his usual smile.

It wasn't long before my brother came in and sat down with us. "Everyone in town is looking for you, Brother. They thought you wandered off somewhere."

"Hell, I'm not lost; I'm with the sheriff. I couldn't be in better hands."

I said goodbye to Denny, and my brother and I drove back to the school and told everyone that I had been found. Later, we drove home to get dressed for the night's gala events — a banquet at the school and, later, a dance at the fire station.

The first person I met when we all walked into the school was one of my old classmates, Judy Cantrell. "Hello, Rosie, you handsome dude. I heard you were in town. I've been waiting here to see you. How in the world are you?"

"I'm well, Judy. Gee, it's good to see you. I told my sisters that this whole trip would be worthwhile if only I got to see you. You are just as lovely as you used to be."

"You haven't changed a bit, Rosie. I've known some people who were good with the 'B.S.,' but you are an artist. Time has sure been good to you. I would have known you anywhere."

I don't remember what we ate at the banquet — I was so busy shaking hands and talking with old friends. The evening passed too quickly, and soon everyone was leaving for the dance at the fire station. Our old friends, Carl Brollier and his wife Shirley, saved a table for us, and we were soon joined by more friends.

"Say something Cajun for us, Larry," one of them said.

"You see my pig down by de bayou, you push him home, yeah? He been gone three day now. Yesterday, today and tomorrow," I said, with the best Cajun accent I could muster.

"Hey, that's great. I wouldn't know you from a real native," Carl said. "I have a bottle of Canadian Mist here, Larry. Would you like a drop?"

"Thanks so much, Carl, but I am on medication that won't allow me to drink. By the way, have you seen our old friend George Rosel lately?" I asked.

"No, I haven't. Not in five or six months. I would sure like to see him while I'm here. I worked for his company for eight or ten years. He gave me a job when I got out of the military, and everything I have become is partially because of him. If you see him soon, tell him I'm sorry I missed him. He was always a good friend."

The evening was over much too soon, and we went home, my mind reeling from all the activities of the day. I had to get to sleep, though. I had to leave tomorrow morning.

During breakfast the next morning, my sister Lois asked me if Stella and I could come to a family reunion on the weekend before Labor Day. It was being held at the little town of Blue Eye, Arkansas, not too far from my cabin.

"That sounds great," I said. "We will certainly work toward that end. Who will be there?"

"Your favorite uncle," Lois said.

"Count me out, then. I don't want to be around him."

"I know you don't care for him, but I never knew why."

"Do you remember after the War, when he came to live with us on the farm? I was about eight years old then. Well, I had a pet pigeon. Remember? Pigeon was a real pet to me, and he used to follow me around like a dog. We went everywhere together. We were as poor as church mice and couldn't afford a dog then. Remember?

"How well I remember," said Lois.

"Pigeon disappeared one day. I looked for him for a week. Couldn't find him anywhere. Mother finally told me that my Uncle had hauled him away. He didn't like Pigeon; he said he was too messy." Mom would feed Pigeon an egg every morning on top of an old barrel out in the yard. My uncle thought he made too much of a mess while he was eating, so he just took him away. "I have never gotten over that."

"That was almost 50 years ago, Brother."

"I remember it like it was yesterday," I told her.

"Please don't let that stop you. You won't even have to talk to him. Don't let one person stop you from seeing everyone else that you want to see."

"We'll see," I said. "I have to be going. I want to stop at the cemetery in Liberal and say hello to Nancy."

Everyone came outside to see me off. "Call if you have any problems," my sister told me.

I drove on to the cemetery at Liberal and, although I had been there only two days before, it took me some time to find Nancy's grave. It was Memorial Day, and the place was full of people putting flowers on graves. Nancy's grave was covered with flowers. Her mom and dad must have been there earlier.

"Hi, Nancy. It's been a long time. I don't get out this way too much anymore, but I know you're okay. I got your signal." We had planted a sweet olive tree in the backyard at our house in Louisiana. Nancy wanted to plant it. She said when it blooms, the smell of the blossoms are just great. It grew for seven or eight years; never bloomed once. Three days after Nancy died, the sweet olive was in full bloom, and the scent was everywhere. You couldn't go outside without smelling it. It was October seventh. I called it my "Resurrection Tree." Obscurantism has never been one of my shortcomings. I hope the day never comes when I will become opposed to enlightenment about the world beyond.

The people who saw me talking to her must have thought I had really lost it but, what the hell, it made me feel better. I would give everything I own to sit and talk to her for just one more hour.

"I'll be seeing you before too long, Nancy. They tell me this thing in my head is terminal. Just another few years. Don't give up on me; I'll be there soon." I had tears in my eyes when I left there, and a lump in my throat that made it hard to swallow.

I had decided to stop for the night in Oklahoma City, but it was still early, and I was feeling good, so I drove on. My thoughts turned to the past. A man works relentlessly to build security — nevermind the cost to himself. Now fate has turned my refuge into a prison. This prison is not a metaphor. It is real, very real.

My mind was in turmoil, and the feeling of uncertainty, almost fear, was gnawing at my stomach. I stared through the windshield at nothing in particular. I was nearing the Arkansas line. I saw a Texaco sign ahead and, since I had a Texaco credit card, I decided to stop for gas. I pulled off the interstate and into the station to the gas pump. I filled the tank and went inside to pay. The girl took my credit card, looked at it, and said, "This is not a Texaco. We can't take this card."

She had a pleasant enough face, but her voice had an edge of arrogance that I found offensive. It was one of those days.

"What other credit cards do you take?" I asked.

"None," she said, her voice getting louder.

There was a policeman standing nearby, having his afternoon coffee break. "Is there a problem here?"

"Nothing I can't fix. Here's money." I handed her my money clip. "Take all you need," I said. I was so shook up, I could hardly talk.

"I see you have a medical alert bracelet. Are you a diabetic?" the policeman asked.

"I wish. My problem is mental...memory...Alzheimer's."

That the word "Alzheimer's" meant something to him was immediately obvious. "Let's have some coffee, Son, and settle down a bit. I'll move your truck to the parking area. Put his coffee on my tab, Darlin'," he told the girl behind the counter, and walked out the door to move my truck. When he came back inside, he sat down and talked with me for nearly an hour. "Do you need me to call someone?" he asked.

"Everyone I know is far away," I said. "My place is not too far from here. I think I can make it there." I heard his life history, and I think he heard mine. It seems his mother was an Alzheimer's patient long ago. By the time I left, I was able to talk and walk again. He told me his name, but I didn't write it down and, try as I might, I can't remember what it was. But I still remember that day when a good public servant helped me through a difficult experience and helped me on my way. God bless him. He has restored some of my faith in the system. I hope to meet him again someday.

The sun was just setting behind the mountains to the west when I got back to the cabin. It was still light enough to see without the headlights. I couldn't believe what I was seeing. Why had I not noticed it before? How long had it been there? I stopped the truck and ran to have a closer look. Yes, sure enough, it was red fern. Red fern was growing all around the foundation of the cabin. I was so happy, I was in tears once again. All of the old hill people will tell you, "Red fern only grows where angels plant it." The angels must love this place as much as I, or was it another sign from Nancy? I'll take it either way.

I went right to bed. I couldn't begin to tell anyone how happy I was at that moment. ℂ

☾

*C*hapter *18*

RETURNS

Stella and I went to the reunion in Blue Eye late that summer. She has to travel with me wherever I go, since the doctors in New Orleans cautioned that I shouldn't drive alone anymore. Not that I'm a bad driver; it's just that I'm taking a chance on getting lost.

My two sisters and my brother-in-law, Sy, were there and, of course, my uncle. I said a quick hello and never talked to him again. He's an old man now, and I would never have recognized him had it not been at that time and place. I did talk to his wife, though— such a nice person. She kissed me when they left. How she put up with him all these years is beyond me; I guess there is no accounting for taste.

All in all, we had a great time. It's not just a family reunion anymore. It's a whole town reunion. Everyone who ever lived there comes back on that day each August. It's quite an event.

That afternoon, Stella and I drove back to the cabin. We took our time, stopping at little antique stores along the way. We stayed there another two or three days, cleaning up, mowing the meadow and weed-eating, taking care not to harm the red fern, of course.

We left early the next morning, before the sun came up. Stella was driving; Floyd was in the back, looking out over the tailgate of the pickup. Not far from the cabin, standing in the road, were two deer— a buck and a doe. They wouldn't move, and Stella had to honk the horn. They walked slowly into the meadow as we passed by. "I'll be back. Some day, some way, I'll be back, you beautiful creatures," I said to them. "I'll be back," I said to myself.

We drove on down the road a few miles. "Remember this place, Stella?"

"Of course, Larry. This is where we saw the eagle. He flew right over the top of the car. I think he was trying to pick up some food in the ditch."

"He sure was big, wasn't he?"

"Sure was. We almost hit him, remember?"

"Yes. I'm glad we didn't. We might see him again, another day." ◖

☾

Chapter 19

To Be Like Him...

I have always admired President Roosevelt for his ability to over-come his handicap and go on with his day-to-day activities as if he wasn't bothered by the fact that he was confined to a wheelchair. Something that would totally devastate a lesser person didn't seem to impact him. I'd like to be like him.

Alzheimer's is not a word you hear every day (unlike AIDS, which you hear about regularly, and which has its own constitu-tion and civil rights). Alzheimer's, it appears, has no agenda in government. It has no "in-your-face" advocates. I'm not even sure it is a disease. It's just a *thing*, a word. It's not caused by a virus or a bacteria. It just is. It's an enigma; and it keeps the afflicted from exerting any control over their own destiny.

I met a man at an auction in Arkansas the other day. He asked me what I did for a living. I told him that I was retired, and that I was writing a book.

"What is the subject of your book?" he asked.

"Alzheimer's."

"And how did you decide on Alzheimer's for a topic?"

"It was something that just popped into my head," I said, with a smile.

"How nice. My mother has Alzheimer's. I'm glad someone is getting the word out. I'll be looking forward to reading your book."

How nice? I thought. He doesn't know I have it. If *he* can't tell, maybe *no one* can.

The fact is that I *do* have it, and I will *still* have it tomorrow when I wake up. I understand that there are 19 different drug studies going on all over the world right now, aimed at relieving the symptoms of Alzheimer's. I'm participating in one of them — along with a thousand others like me. We are on the cutting edge of research. There are dangers, but it is also dangerous to do nothing. I have been a mover and a shaker all my life. I can't just sit and do nothing. I want to be like President Roosevelt in that respect. I want to press on for as long as I have the mental ability.

There have been many changes in my life since the onset of Alzheimer's, some for which I am not at all ungrateful. I have more compassion for people, birds, deer, and the like. I have fallen more and more in love with Stella.

Although I feel good about myself at times, I strive to remember that, merely because I sometimes feel more at ease, I should not make the mistake of supposing that the danger is over. It comes back soon enough. My thoughts become jumbled, progressing to complete disorientation and confusion, and my speech becomes garbled or slow. The words that once came so fluently must now be thought about for some time. I avoid conversation when I'm in this state of confusion. Past events, as well as recent ones, are often forgotten, and my ability to do everyday tasks is gravely impaired. I work my mind harder now than ever before.

Besides Stella and my support group at the cafe, I have one other support system — God.

I think most people believe in God, although the beliefs are diverse. Some think of God as an impersonal energy force who is the universe. Others think of God as a maker of everything, but who is then no longer involved with the Universe that He has created. I suppose that there are as many views of God as there are people.

I personally believe in the Bible's picture of him. He can be a source of hope. He created the universe and everything in it, and He is still active in it, and with all that He has created, including me. If I didn't have a relationship with God, I couldn't go on.

I believe that this life is not the end of everything, that there is another life beyond, a life where there is no death, no cancer, no tears and, I am sure, no Alzheimer's. I am sure that, when my life is over, this dark cloud in my mind will be gone forever.

My thoughts drift back to the Alzheimer's patients I have seen in nursing homes, just lying there, gone, for all intents and purposes. Can they still think? What are their thoughts? Are they closer to God than we will ever know? Closer than you and I?

There is so much to do, so little time. My doctors tell me that I am on what is called a "plateau." I am no better, but no worse. I could stay on this plateau for ten years or ten minutes. There is no way of telling. I am going to live every minute like it was my last.

If my condition should worsen, no one can say I didn't give life everything I had, that I didn't try everything possible.

There are many people in the world whom I still haven't met. I must get busy. If you are one of the people whom I haven't met, I'm sorry; it's my loss.

If, when you read this book, you feel a certain sadness, as some have told me they did, let yourself be sad, but not for me. Let yourself feel for all sick people. I have had a good and prosperous life. I have done it all, and I have enjoyed it. If I die tonight, I won't be cheated out of anything. Most of all, I have had the love of some beautiful people... and I have loved them, too. ◖

☾

Chapter 20

AFTERWORD
Stella Guidry

I have been entrusted to write the last chapter of this story about the very special person in my life. And, yes, he is special. Larry has a wonderful heart, one that is open to everyone he meets, two-legged as well as four-legged.

When I first met Larry, I was immediately introduced to his dog Joe and to the Westie Nancy left behind. I noticed right away how they greeted each other. I remember thinking to myself, this man has such a delightful way with his dog, I have to get to know him.

He was the first man I had met, after the death of my husband, who had such a presence about him regarding the dignity of women. If he treats his female dog this way, he must hold women, in general, as precious. I was right. As our relationship matured, we both realized that, at some point in time, we had been soul mates. There was just too much synchronism in our earthly life to even think otherwise.

Each one of us has our own idea of what life should be like. However, sometimes these ideas change, and I, like anyone else, resist change. I like the "comfort zone" in life. In the beginning of our relationship, I really thought I had found someone with whom to spend the rest of my life. Loneliness can be such a dirty word. It is in the psyche of each one of us to resist living alone. That goes back to the beginning of time; it's human.

I remember one particular sunny day, Larry and I were working in the yard, and he was on a ladder, repairing a leaking gutter when he said, "Stel, will you marry me? I love you, and I want to spend the rest of my life with you."

"In due time, Larry, in due time," I responded.

He, in turn, said, "I want you to know that I will only ask you ten more times, and then that will be it; I will not ask again."

"Larry," I said, "I will let you know when I'm ready. I need to be sure about this before we take any more steps toward a commitment for life. I have to be really in love, not only with my heart, but with my head, too."

He had given me an engagement ring the previous Christmas, asking for my hand in marriage, the old-fashioned way, on his knees. I said, "Yes, one day, Larry." At that time, I was not ready for marriage, but wanted the option kept open with this man. His sense of humor was something I so desperately needed. I was coming out of a fog that had blanketed my life for awhile, and the last thing I needed now was to get involved in another heavy relationship. Grief and mourning had almost become a way of life for me.

I have known grief in ways that are quite difficult to describe. The death of a spouse, the death of a family relationship (which is another story), and now, this Alzheimer's thing, which has taken both our lives in a completely different direction.

I am still mourning the loss of Larry's intellect. I miss so much how he used to be. His personality has become more withdrawn now, and the traits that make him who he is, and what he is about, are slowly slipping away. The breathing, the physical functions, are still very much alive, but the living of his life, his normal way of thinking before taking action, is slowly leaving him.

At times, prayer is my only resource, and one that I use quite a bit. Without it, I don't know where I would be today. I think of the day when heavy decisions about his well-being will have to be put into practice. We have taken the necessary legal steps to appropriately care for Larry. His children and I will take those steps when the time comes. But until then, we will live as normal a life as we possibly can, whatever "normal" is.

There are several good guide books on the market for dealing with Alzheimer's patients. Again, whatever works for you, the caregiver, is what you should be doing. There are other important issues that have to be addressed — medical issues; finances; safety; day-by-day, hour-by-hour care and, of course, support for the caregiver. This is one area that the caregiver has to really focus on for, without it, the commitment deteriorates quickly.

In my case, I felt once again that I was losing someone very dear and important to me. I am thankful that I had already done my homework and knew quite well how to take care of myself. I enjoy my creative side and my work. Somehow, this puts me back in touch with the reality of the outside world. I have massages faith-fully, once a month; I eat nourishing food; I have my time-out as often as I possibly can, and I surround myself with good music — the soft, soothing kind. I am not much for television, because it is such a passive activity and can be quite depressing at times. I like to read good books, too; it keeps my focus intact. Because Larry is in the early stages, he is still able to take to the mountains. This gives me time to regroup and regenerate my own sense of self. The last thing we need is for me to fall to pieces. And, honestly, some-times I would like that luxury, but my own personal energy system would suffer. Why not keep the positive energy flowing? Some sense of sanity has to sustain this relationship.

Knowing that someone is depending on me sometimes weighs heavily. Depression is such a loosely used word today, I think it is the stigmatized definition used by the medical profession to label a variety of dis-eases in our culture. I, for one, would use the word depression when I could not pinpoint a cause of dis-ease in myself. I really thought Larry was in a state of depression. I wanted so much to believe *that* — because it's treatable.

Sometimes, I would come home from work, and the house would be pitch dark. I am a person of light; I need light all around me. But Larry would come home first from his day's work, and I would find him asleep on the sofa. I thought this was strange because, in the beginning, he would be up and doing things around the house. Cooking and cleaning was not his forte. However, we had the best-dressed lawn in the neighborhood. He was always in the yard, cleaning, cutting, trimming anything he could get his hands on. Now, it seemed, it was a chore just to start the lawn mower.

I knew in my heart something was wrong. This was not like him. Even our nights out together became further and further apart. Some days, he would just stare into space. Often, there was just no Larry around. It was like someone else was inhabiting the thin, beautiful body and mind of this man I'd found to be so dashing, (especially while holding a tennis racket or a seven iron). His sharpness was fading. We used to talk for hours on end about politics, world affairs, what we both wanted out of life. Those hours are but a memory now. I would come to feed on these times, for those were truly cherished moments.

I remember once telling him, "Larry, I just love hanging out with you. You make me laugh; you make me think; and having you in my life has given new meaning to the word 'living'."

Now, the acuity of his mind has given way to murkiness, which scares me. What have I gotten myself into? How am I going to hold onto this life we both so desperately want? Where will I go for help? It's becoming obvious he cannot control what's happening to him.

And with all the legal ramifications over his "right to live," his "right to die," his right to decide where to go from here — all these questions now enter my own mind when I think of how to help this fifty-something man, this man who has so much more living to do. And then, I think, what would his children do, his family of remaining siblings? How would *they* want to care for him? Do I call them and ask for advice? What about his doctors, and most of all, what about HIM? What does *he* want to do?

I asked him if he wanted to move back to Kansas. He emphatically told me, "NO, not under *any* circumstances. And I do not want to be buried in Houma, Louisiana, either."

That statement resulted in our decision to be buried with our previous spouses. It would make things easier on our children. Quite sensible, I thought. Finally, we were getting somewhere.

Larry is really bonded with his cafe support cronies. There is no way I would allow anyone or anything to sever those relationships. These are important people to him, and I honor each one who provides him with what he needs to face each new day. They each bring a special gift to this man's life. And for that, I am thankful.

I do worry about him driving alone when he decides it's time for the mountains. I can't always take off and go with him; so I just bless him and send him on his way. He needs to feel that he can still do things on his own. So what if he gets lost now and then? His truck is well-equipped with communication and identification devices, and he is well identified with Safe-Return. Why not allow him this little luxury? Soon enough, this will cease. And then... ?

It is this, "and then..." that keeps me in darkness. I know I can survive one way or another. It is my wish and my prayer that I can keep my own faculties afloat long enough to see him through this Alzheimer's hex, for lack of a better word.

Once the diagnosis was made, we were both in shock, to say the least. You think things like this happen to others, not to you. It is important to point out here that a cut will heal; some cancers are treatable; and yes, surgery can fix almost anything. But the mind... how do you fix *that?* There are no known drugs approved today to treat Alzheimer's; Cognex appears to help, but there are side effects.

It is horrendous to hear that, once the diagnosis is made, it is just a matter of time before the nursing home enters the picture, and you see, flashing before your eyes, pictures of people lying in bed, with their mouths open, not knowing whether they are here with us, or some place else.

That is the horror of this disease. Where does it come from, and how can it be stopped? Is it in the air we breathe, the water we drink, or the food we eat? Countless other diseases are directly related to these elements. What about heredity? What about our children? How do we protect them? Can we? These are all questions that need answers, and in our lifetime. And coping. How do we, as caregivers, cope? Do we look on care as a job? It is gradually coming to this. I try to give Larry as much freedom and support as I possibly can, with supervision, of course. The last thing I want to do is create a cripple. That is no way for any person to live.

I encourage him to continue his drug therapy, because he has to. He has to stay involved; he is entirely too young to submit to this horror with out a fight. Maybe, just maybe, having him involved with his own treatment will help to slow the impact of the disease on his mind.

In the beginning, when the first diagnosis was made, I told him that we would not take this sitting down. We would search for some type of program to involve ourselves in. I was holding out hope to a man who had no hope. I told him that all that was needed was to find answers, no matter what it took. We decided to chance drug therapy. Now, at least we are *doing* something. We are not sitting back, waiting for the progression of this disease.

It takes guts to ingest a drug that no one but the drug company knows anything about; to chance having a healthy physical body one day, and the next, being totally disabled. It is a scary move to make, but one I am thankful, today, that we made. I have seen Larry go from depression, anxiety and tears at times (because he could not find the words to express himself), to intelligent conversation, calmness, and yes, even brightness in his eyes. There are days where he is bouncing off the walls, so to speak, and I reach out and hug him, comfort him, and tell him to calm down. There are days when he is quiet and contemplative. On those days, when I ask, "Are you okay?" sometimes I get an answer, and sometimes I do not. I try to observe as much as I can and, sometimes, even read his mind. I verbalize a lot of what he is thinking as he searches for words that are not there.

Each person is unique, and I have learned that this may not work for everyone. But it is definitely worth a try.

I have read that, sometimes, Alzheimer's patients become violent, but I have not experienced this with Larry. I think each caregiver has to evaluate his/her own situation, to appropriately handle instances of violence. It is difficult to assess situations in advance. Preparation and a plan of action, whether written or held in memory, are the only ways in which each person can deal with Alzheimer's. And, yes, there *are* a lot of "do-gooders" out there, and you *will* come across them. Bite your tongue; listen to what they have to say; and then trust your inside voice to give you what you need to handle the situation. Focus on what you feel is the right thing to do for your patient as well as for yourself. Scream when you need to get out the pent-up emotions. My car is my refuge. I drive with all the windows up, in case I need to scream. I also have a plastic bat that I use on a pillow when things get really out of hand. It has been a long time since I used this method, but it works. It keeps the emotions on tap, and believe me, this is important to an Alzheimer's caregiver.

At some point in time, we will have to consider home care and long-term care. We are still in the early stages with this Alzheimer's monkey and, hopefully, we have a few good years left to enjoy our lives together. We are doing just that, as much as we possibly can. Keeping the focus on today is difficult, at best, but we have to, simply because today is all we really have. Today, we will laugh, love, and lighten the load for ourselves; and we will pass through the pain, the heartache and sometimes, the loneliness that comes with this thing called Alzheimer's. No one is immune to this deadly disease. It can happen to any one of us.

In this manner, we get to the "art" of living a life within circumstances beyond our control. It is how we get through it all that matters. In my heart, I know that there is a bigger picture where we all are connected. My faith has sustained me thus far, and my faith is my drawing card today. I will continue this walk I started with Larry until that day comes when one of us will say goodbye. One of us will be sad, but we will have known that the passage to another life is life-giving. I, for one, do not want to look back and say, "I should have..." I hope to have fought the good fight, and, not have to come back to learn the lessons I haven't yet learned. Rest is my ultimate goal. ❰

☾

The author, Larry Rose,
may be contacted at the address below:

Larry Rose
P.O. Box 81321
Lafayette LA 70598

OTHER RESOURCES FROM ELDER BOOKS

Gone Without A Trace by Marianne Caldwell

Stella Dickerman, an accomplished artist and weaver, vanished mysteriously on September 13, 1991, two years after the onset of Alzheimer's disease. *Gone Without A Trace* is the gripping personal story of her daughter's quest for answers during the long search odyssey which ensued. A first-of-its-kind, *Gone Without A Trace* provides unique insight into the profound pain endured by the families of missing persons, and offers sensitive guidance on how to comfort them.

$10.95

Surviving Alzheimer's: A Guide for Families
by Florian Raymond

Easily digestible, this book is a treasure house of practical tips, ideas and survival strategies for the busy caregiver. It describes how to renew and restore yourself during the ups and downs of caregiving, and shows you how to take care of yourself as well as your family member.

$10.95

Failure-Free Activities for the Alzheimer's Patient
by Carmel Sheridan

This award-winning book describes hundreds of simple, non-threatening activities which are suitable for persons with Alzheimer's disease. The author describes how to focus on the abilities that remain rather than the patient's deficits and shows how to create activities which capitalize on existing strengths.

$10.95

Reminiscence: Uncovering A Lifetime of Memories
by Carmel Sheridan

Reminiscing is one of the most powerful healing activities for people with Alzheimer's disease. This book explains the simple techniques involved in stimulating memories. It outlines themes to explore, as well as hundreds of meaningful activities involving reminiscence.

$12.95

ORDER FORM

Send To:

Elder Books   Post Office Box 490   Forest Knolls CA 94933
PH: 1 800 909 COPE (2673)   FAX: 415 488-4720

Please send me:

Qty.		Price/copy	Totals
____	*Show Me the Way to Go Home*	@ *$10.95*	$____.__
____	*Gone Without A Trace*	@ *$10.95*	$____.__
____	*Surviving Alzheimer's:* *A Guide for Families*	@ *$10.95*	$____.__
____	*Failure-Free Activities*	@ *$10.95*	$____.__
____	*Reminiscence*	@ *$12.95*	$____.__

Total for books . . . . $____.__

Total sales tax . . . . $____.__

Total shipping . . . . $____.__

Amount enclosed . . . . $____.__

Shipping: $2.50 for first book, $1.25 for each additional book;
California residents, please add 8.25% sales tax.

_____
Name

_____
Address

_____
City   State   Zip